Praise for *Be Your Ow*

'There is no such thing as a born leader. We all have to learn, both from our own experiences and the wisdom of others. Exercising leadership, in any field of endeavour, can be challenging, and sometimes even daunting, but there are few privileges greater than being given the opportunity to lead others and to make a difference. Karen Stein has written an invaluable book, full of wisdom and practical experience that will help you to be the leader who inspires others to reach their potential. I wish I had been given such insights as I travelled on my own leadership journey. I recommend it highly.'

Lieutenant General David Morrison AO (Retd)

'Karen Stein has written one of the most comprehensive and practical guides for leaders I've ever read. Through engaging, evidence-based and high-impact practices, you'll learn to lead yourself, lead others and leave a lasting legacy. *Be Your Own Leadership Coach* isn't a book you simply read, it's a book you *experience* and become better because of it.'

Zach Mercurio, PhD, author of *The Invisible Leader: Transform Your Life, Work, and Organization with the Power of Authentic Purpose*

'*Be Your Own Leadership Coach* is full of practical advice and tools that I have already started applying to my life. The backpack metaphor works for me. I recommend this book to anyone who is seeking to improve their personal and professional life.'

Sergio Duchini, Chair, Lymphoma Australia

'Written by a wise and gentle leadership coach, *Be Your Own Leadership Coach* is an easy to read and comprehensive self-help guide for anyone wanting to become a better version of themselves at work. Drawing on research, stories and a wealth of personal experience, Karen provides the why as well as the how-to of self-development, with lots of practical exercises.'

Dr Juliet Bourke, advisor, board member and Professor of Practice, School of Management & Governance, UNSW Business School

'In a world calling for leaders who can simultaneously hold space for courage and kindness, *Be Your Own Leadership Coach* disrupts the traditional dominance and power of what it means to 'lead' and makes the compelling case for 'whole human' leadership development that starts from within. A must-read for anyone driven to create real impact in today's ever-changing world!'

Mariane Power, clinical psychologist, female founder – The Posify Group

'I could not think of a better person to write a book on coaching than Karen. Her characteristic warmth resonates on every page and in every strategy and story. Karen has reminded us that we can lead and learn to be and do better in any given moment.'

Kelly Irving, book coach, editor and Founder of The Expert Author Community

SELF-COACHING STRATEGIES
TO LEAD *YOUR* WAY

Be Your Own Leadership Coach

KAREN STEIN

MAJOR
STREET

First published in 2023 by Major Street Publishing Pty Ltd
info@majorstreet.com.au | +61 421 707 983 | majorstreet.com.au

 A catalogue record for this book is available
from the National Library of Australia

Printed book ISBN: 978-1-922611-75-8
Ebook ISBN: 978-1-922611-76-5

Cover design by Simone Geary
Internal design by Production Works
Printed by IVE

10 9 8 7 6 5 4 3 2 1

Contents

Preface

Many leaders dream of having a leadership coach: a dedicated cheerleader and confidant to support their thinking and development, and help them explore their issues and concerns. They imagine a coach helping them increase their self-awareness of their behaviours, emotions and cognitions, and the impact they have on them personally and on those they lead. They picture someone working with them through the many expected and unexpected challenges of leadership – someone who enables them to be their best selves so they can have the leadership impact they hope for.

The great news is, there are plenty of leadership coaches to choose from. It is estimated that there are more than 71,000 coaches globally, with 30 per cent of these coaches describing themselves as leadership coaches and 65 per cent as business coaches.[1] So, based on numbers alone, you are likely to be able to identify a coach to meet your needs.

As an Executive Coach, I can't agree more with the benefits of engaging with a coach. Not only have I had my own coach, I continue to seek coaching through group coaching and coaching supervision. I am also actively engaged in coaching business leaders, as well as women who are hoping to re-enter the workplace after time away from employment. The growth and development I witness in those I coach is always exciting and motivating.

What you may not realise is that it's also possible to have a coach with you on tap – someone who you can access at any time, with no waiting or scheduling required. This leadership coach is well known to you, and is there to support you day by day, step by step and in the moment. In fact, you know your coach better than most. This coach, my friend, is *you*!

As your own coach you'll have access to your own self-coaching strategies. You won't be waiting for your next appointment with your external coach to better yourself, nor will you be left wondering how to tackle your leadership issues between sessions. This book will help you fill your virtual backpack with self-coaching strategies to support your self-leadership and leadership of others. The strategies in this book focus on helping you lead *your* way so that you can have the influence you desire – creating a positive, long-lasting impact that continues in your absence.

After reading this book, my hope is that, as you prepare to start your work each day, you'll strap on your virtual backpack loaded with your self-coaching strategies. You'll carry it around with you, leaving the flap loosely tied so you can slip your hand in and draw out whichever strategy is appropriate as you face your leadership tasks. In some cases, the strategy you select will support you in being your best self; in other cases, it will support you as you lead others.

By working through the exercises in this book and applying the strategies within, you'll learn to recognise what is helping you and hindering you in the moment. You'll be more attuned to your own effectiveness and able to support and rescue yourself to ensure your continued success.

A trusted partner in your self-coaching discovery

As an experienced International Coaching Federation Professional Certified Coach and senior leader with more than 30 years' professional services experience – including 23 years as a Partner of Deloitte – I am here to build these strategies with you.

As I approached my halfway point (I was getting closer to 50 and am determined to live to 100!), I reflected on how I could live out my chapter two in an impactful way. At around the same time I was fortunate to be provided with a coach while on an executive leadership program, and I fell head over heels in love with the process of coaching. It was fabulous! I knew that coaching would allow me to support others to be their best selves and help me to live the impactful, purposeful life I sought.

In 2016, I pivoted into my second career within Deloitte as a Talent Partner and Executive Coach. I provide executive leadership coaching to evolving senior leaders, supporting them to achieve their professional goals. I also designed and lead the Executive Coaching Program for Women Partners of Deloitte, and co-facilitate other leadership programs.

My experience as a senior leader within a professional services environment means I was, for a long time, on your side of the page of this book. I was a leader hoping to bring her best self to her team, her clients, her community and of course herself. Additionally, I wanted to be a role model for the young people in my life. I was hopeful I could help them see leadership in a positive light and guide them as the young leaders and wonderful humans they are.

Leadership can be challenging, frustrating, frightening and overwhelming, but it can also be delightful, fulfilling, engaging and exciting! How you approach it and how you respond to it will draft your leadership story.

I discovered early in my leadership career that the more I discovered about myself, the more positive my leadership impact could be. This set me on a path of learning about who I am, how I relate to others and how I engage with myself. It was only later, in my senior years of leadership, that I became excited about the power of coaching. It opened my mind to new ways of thinking – new perspectives, insights and understanding – which better enabled me to have the impact I hoped for.

Once I trained as an Executive Coach I felt strongly that I wanted to use my newfound knowledge to make a difference in the world.

I am fortunate to work with inspiring leaders each day with varied backgrounds, goals, dreams and challenges. I also provide voluntary coaching to clients of Dress for Success and the social enterprise Bambuddha Group. This book is another way for me to encourage equitable access to coaching and bring these powerful coaching strategies to more people. Coaching leaders to be their best selves improves their wellbeing, which ripples to that of their teams, organisations and communities. Step by step this makes our world a better place.

In this book I draw on evidence-based positive psychology as well as my lived leadership experience and more than 2000 hours of one-on-one coaching. Together we'll set you up to approach your leadership journey with confidence, optimism and a strong sense of self. My hope in writing this book is to enable you, as a leader, to pause and reflect on what your leadership impact is and can be. You too can positively impact our world.

Join me as we build your leadership self-coaching strategies together.

Introduction

'Tell me, why should I read this book?' This is a question I've been asked many times as I've shared my excitement about getting ink on the page. What is the problem my reader might be trying to resolve, and how might this book help them?

During your leadership journey you have likely considered the type of leader you want to be. What impact would you like to have, and how will you achieve this? You probably want to be the best leader you can be and have a positive impact on others (and yourself). However, no one has told you *how* to do this. You may be concerned that you *should* know what to do, you *should* know how to lead. Yet it's not that simple. You don't know what you don't know, but you must work it out if you're to become a confident, empowered and impactful leader.

You may feel a little anxious or vulnerable in this space. Many leaders seek outside support to help them manage this. Leadership coaching is a powerful medium to generate exploration and self-discovery. It allows for learning and growth with the creation of new knowledge, insights and understanding. When you engage with a coach you are entering a safe space where you can consider how to develop the skills, behaviours, emotions and thoughts that will support your achievement of professional goals. I provide those I coach with this judgement-free space where they can consider options to work towards success, navigate obstacles and form new insights.

Inevitably, though, coaching sessions last for a finite period. What happens once the coaching comes to an end? What happens when you can't access a coach in the moment you need one? What if you can't access coaching at all for financial or practical reasons? How do you support yourself?

This is where you need to become your best coach. It's where I – and this book – can help you!

In this book I present 12 practices to be your best coach. Within these pages you'll discover when to use each practice and the value each brings. You'll be equipped to lead *your* way: in support of yourself and in support of others.

Your leadership will evolve over time, and the trajectory of your success will rise when you invest in yourself. By mindfully engaging in self-coaching using the strategies in this book, you'll learn to pay attention to the impact you're having on yourself and others. You will become more intentional and deliberate in how you lead. You will build your self-awareness and sense of self so you are better able to make informed choices as to how you achieve your leadership impact. You will notice more about yourself. You will empower yourself to draw on coaching strategies *in the moment* as your leadership requires this of you. You will become more autonomous, more responsive, more confident and more informed. All of this will assist you with leading your way, with impact, as your best self.

Leadership is not a title

Before we unpack the concept of self-coaching, let's take a look at what it actually means to lead. Most of our conversations around leadership in a professional context tend to focus on the efficacy of a particular leader: 'My CEO is awesome. She is an exceptional leader,' or, 'Our Managing Director is not much of a leader.'

We often reference leaders in positions of power: the C-suite, management, operations or business unit leaders. We use titles to recognise leadership. We talk of people being leaders based on their role description or where they sit in an organisational structure. We send executives on leadership courses to build their leadership skills, and we train experienced hires to *become* leaders. We seek promotions so we can attain leadership positions, badging ourselves as chiefs, officers, presidents and directors, high up in the organisational pecking order.

These corporate leadership positions have titles that originated deep in the history of power and authority. From the military world of generals and officers to the political world of presidents and vice presidents, these titles bestow high esteem and denote those who require followers to succeed. A chief is defined as 'the head or leader of a body of people; the person highest in authority'.[2] The 'organisational chief' concept is growing. Google searches reveal a plethora of 'chief' titles including Chief Executive Officer, Chief Financial Controller, Chief Operating Officer, Chief Human Resources Officer, Chief Marketing Officer, Chief Digital Officer and – my personal favourite – Chief Happiness Officer. The possibilities for leadership roles seem only to be growing!

A common view of leadership is that it lives only in the heights of organisations, where those in the know, or those with significant tenure and experience, are *placed* into positions of leadership. What we often overlook is that leadership is not limited to positional leadership. We are *all* leaders, regardless of our position.

Leadership is an act, a practice, a set of behaviours that can be adopted at *all* stages of life and in *any* situation. It is a culmination of who you are and who you have become. It's present at every step throughout your working life.

Leading yourself to lead others

Leadership can be hard. You must take a thoughtful approach to acknowledge and manage the many thoughts and emotions that arise along the way. You might get in your own way, overthink or over-complicate things, or lose your confidence. You might rely on your instincts to guide you, yet not notice how your perspective is distorted. You might overlook feedback, move on too quickly and not realise how you have affected others until it is too late. You might make time for everyone besides yourself and be too busy to stop, reflect and notice what's happening.

Consider too the world we live in, the system in which you form a part. During your leadership journey you will grapple with volatility, uncertainty, complexity and ambiguity on a global, local and micro scale. Filling your virtual backpack with self-coaching strategies will enable you to better respond to the ever-changing systems surrounding you. Systems theorists tell us that a linear leadership path is unlikely to be found in the future; rather, your leadership path will be revealed as you experience the changing dynamics and what emerges.

With this in mind, it is okay to feel somewhat concerned about how to be the best leader you can be. Leading in a volatile system can require big thinking. But it's so worth it! The system you belong to is not straightforward or programmatic. Your experience of it may feel uncomfortable and awkward, unpredictable and unscripted. Success will require you to heighten your awareness as to what is possible and what you can influence, and the likely consequences (intended and unintended) of the leadership decisions you make. Despite the challenges, leading in this environment can be exciting, stimulating and engaging.

Achieving leadership success in an ever-changing world requires you to lead yourself well. Leading yourself is a process of learning to honour your values, utilise your strengths and fulfil your purpose. You lead yourself to design goals, fulfil goals and change your goals. You lead yourself by choosing priorities and making choices that move you closer to the outcomes you want and away from outcomes you don't. You lead yourself to have an impact and to find fulfilment so you can live a purposeful, meaningful life. You lead *your* way.

Your personal leadership may require refinement and development. At times you may struggle to lead yourself appropriately. You may ignore your shortcomings or overlook development opportunities. You may lack self-awareness and perspective. You may wonder how you can better your self-leadership to allow you to make better choices, be more fulfilled and have greater meaning and impact in what you select to do.

Once you coach yourself to build and widen your perspective, enter into quality communication and dialogue, seek feedback and grow your self-awareness, you will be better placed to have the impact you want. You will have what you need to advance, empower, grow, influence and support others. How you do so will be reflective of you. You will need to be aware of how *you* refine your leadership skills as you lead others. You will need to focus on your visibility, how you are perceived and your behaviour towards others so you can build trust. You will need to consider how you communicate and listen as you engage with others and lead your way.

Once you adopt the 12 practices and related strategies outlined in this book, you will have instant access to a new repertoire of skills, behaviours, emotions and thoughts to support you. You will have found your leadership coach – in *yourself*.

Becoming an impactful leader

If you want to be the best leader you can be, you must consider the impact you want to have on others and for yourself. Sheryl Sandberg, quoting Harvard Business School Professor Frances Frei, said, 'Leadership is about making others better as a result of your presence and making sure that impact lasts in your absence.'[3] The essence of this quote is that leadership requires your presence beyond your physical form. Your leadership presence is shaped by how you make people feel, what they hear from you and what they see you do. This presence has an enduring impact that lasts in your absence.

Your leadership impact is the impression you make that inspires and motivates others to be their best selves. It's the perception you create to generate optimism and hope. It's the positive effect you have on others through your role modelling of behaviours, emotions and thoughts. It's building confidence and commitment in others. It's your ability to make people feel like they truly matter. To understand and support those around you requires empathy and compassion, as well as listening skills to learn and consider new and diverse perspectives. An impactful leader utilises open and courageous communication to share their vision and a common purpose, embrace innovation and creativity, delineate goals and priorities, and include and collaborate.

This may sound overwhelming; however, it is only when you leave it to chance, fate or destiny that it is so. To have this leadership impact, this enduring presence, relies on you first leading yourself. The more that you become conscious of how you see yourself and how you behave, think and feel, the easier it will be to determine and influence how you impact others.

Conscious leadership is impactful leadership. As a conscious leader, you are aware of how you engage with others, you notice how you make them feel and, as a result, you build trust and strong relationships. It's even better when you notice how *you* behave, how *you* feel and how *you* think. When you're attuned to your behaviours, emotions and thoughts, you're better placed to recognise which of these you want to draw upon or alter to help you achieve your intended impact. You will become more mindful of the choices you can make to support your leadership.

When approached with a mindful stance, leadership can be energising, fulfilling, challenging and rewarding. Adopting self-coaching strategies will support you in bringing your best self forward as a leader. You can then lead others and have your desired impact, as shown in Figure 1.

Figure 1: Leading yourself to lead others and achieve impact

You're sure to be familiar with the notion of applying your own oxygen mask before helping others around you. It's the same with leadership. The greater your ability to lead yourself, the more impactful you are likely to be when leading others. When you support yourself you are building your leadership core: the strength and courage to lead from within as your authentic self, which can then be utilised to lead others. This is how you will build your leadership impact, and it will be advanced as you utilise self-coaching strategies.

The magic of self-coaching

When my former coachee, Nell, emailed me it had been more than 12 months since our last scheduled coaching session. We hadn't had much contact since, but I have always encouraged my coachees to contact me should they need additional support. My eyes flashed across Nell's email in anticipation as I wondered what support she might require. My instincts told me there may be a number of areas in which she may be seeking support. I reflected on the numerous conversations in which we had explored solutions to leadership issues she was experiencing. During my time working with Nell, she experimented with and learnt from the strategies we discussed while building her self-awareness around her communication style. We had concluded our last scheduled session by identifying the areas in which she intended to further grow and develop.

As I returned my attention to Nell's email my heart warmed and my smile grew. I was delighted to read that Nell had experienced several *leadership choice points,* as I like to call them: moments when she made a significant decision that would impact her and her team. Rather than seeking me out for additional coaching, she was proudly sharing how she had drawn on her self-coaching strategies to support herself. During our time working together we had filled her virtual backpack with self-coaching strategies to steer her through moments like these. She had mastered the art of reaching into her backpack and selecting the appropriate strategy to utilise to be her best self and achieve her desired leadership impact.

Nell wrote about how she had practised self-reflection, preparation, deliberation and consultation with others. She shared feedback from her team that reflected their gratitude and high regard for her in supporting them through difficult times. Best of all, she felt empowered in herself. I could feel her success radiating through the email. She had led herself, she had led others and she had had a positive leadership impact – enduring beyond her presence with her team.

My intention with this book is to help you build *your* skills in self-coaching, just as I did with Nell. Self-coaching is a skill that requires practice and attention. It is not something you try on and have it fit comfortably the first time. It requires reflection, consideration and adjustment to best suit your needs.

Of course, you can also engage an experienced and well-qualified external coach to support your self-coaching if that option is available to you. This is the approach my coachee Nell, and many others like her, have taken. My book is intended to guide you to build your own self-coaching skills, which can then be supplemented with support from a qualified coach to enhance your discovery of alternative perspectives, reflections and insights.

The more that you invest in yourself – through both self-coaching and external coaching – the more you'll be supported to better understand your assumptions, reactions, beliefs and behaviours, and the more comfortably you will lead as your best self.

The benefits of self-coaching are many:

- You will be less reliant on hindsight to teach you and correct your ways. Instead, you will use foresight to make considered decisions about how you lead.

- As you become more connected with your choices and responses, you will truly *experience* more of your leadership. I refer to this as *being* a leader, rather than just *doing* leadership.

- You will become more empowered, confident and reflective. You will be more attentive to your potential as you grow and develop through self-coaching.

- You will learn more about yourself. You'll learn about what you do well and what might require further development. You'll learn what engages and excites you, and what drags you down. You'll learn how to solve issues and lean into challenges, and when to seek support from others. You will get to know yourself even better than you do now.

- You'll learn to respond faster. Once you have mastered the self-coaching strategies, you'll be more adept at drawing on them more readily. You'll know where to find them in your backpack and will keep your favourite strategies near the top!

- Your learnings will ripple to your team, clients, customers, family and friends. You will positively impact others with your heightened understanding of yourself and your leadership impact. You will make this world a better place.

Self-coaching requires some things from you:

- *Self-reflection:* You will need to make time to draw your attention to how you are behaving, thinking or feeling in a given situation. This requires you to observe yourself objectively as an outsider might.

- *Self-assessment:* After reflecting, you will need to assess what is helping you and what is hindering you in relation to your objective. Which of your identified behaviours, emotions and thoughts are helpful and which are less so in this moment? Which alternative behaviours, emotions and thoughts could better assist you at this time, and what might that look like? What patterns are you noticing that are becoming more evident through ongoing self-assessment? What questions can you ask of yourself to alter your perspective and gain new insights?

- *Experimentation and learning:* Which self-coaching strategies can you put into play to assist you? What might you pull out of your backpack to support you in this moment? Your experimentation and learning can be transformational.

- *Further reflection and action:* What are you noticing of yourself and others as a result of your self-coaching strategy? How is it advancing you towards your positive leadership impact? What might you do more of or less of?

- *Practice:* To move from a novice to mastery-level leader, you will need to practise your self-coaching strategies to improve, grow and develop. It won't happen overnight, but it will happen with practice. This is what will help you lead yourself, lead with others and have the leadership impact you are seeking.

Self-coaching will help you move from uncertainty, hesitation and regret to growth, confidence and impact (see Figure 2).

The process of self-coaching requires you to refrain from leading on autopilot. Rather, you must become connected with your own sense of self as a leader. As you work through the practices you will refine and shape your leadership so you feel most comfortable with how you lead and what you represent. You will soon recognise more leadership choice points and become more accountable and responsible for your own behaviours, emotions and thoughts.

Figure 2: The impact of self-coaching

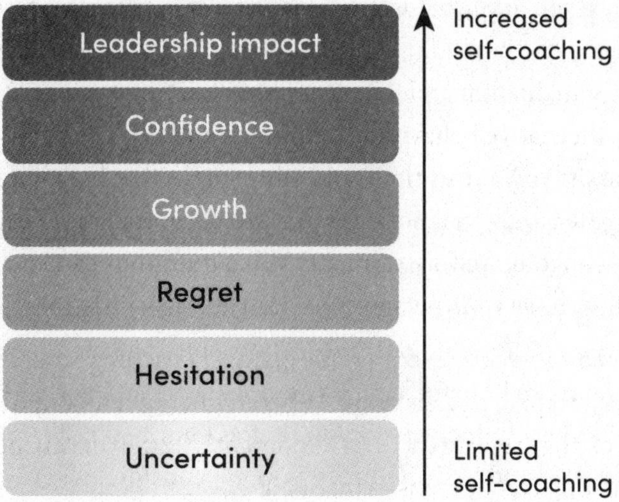

Leadership impact — Increased self-coaching

Confidence

Growth

Regret

Hesitation

Uncertainty — Limited self-coaching

How to use this book

The 12 practices in this book will guide you through the process of self-coaching for leading yourself and self-coaching for leading others. I suggest selecting a notebook to record your responses and work through the exercises within. You can also visit my website – **karensteincoaching.com** – to download an e-journal, which has workspace for your use.

In the first seven practices we'll focus on leading yourself. Self-coaching supports you to lead as your best self – to honour your values, lead with purpose and use your strengths. It helps you confirm why you matter. You will become self-aware of your behaviours, emotions and thoughts, allowing for continuous learning and self-development. You will sooner identify your goals and motivating factors, and grow in confidence and self-belief. You will become better equipped to respond to challenges and solve complex problems, increasing your resilience and mental toughness. Lastly, you will experience improved wellbeing as you experience more positive emotions, hope, optimism and engagement.

In **Practice 1** we'll build your coaching strategies to *lead as you*. By understanding your values, strengths and purpose you will be able to connect (or perhaps reconnect) with your sense of self. This is your true north – your navigational system that will support you as you lead your way. By honouring your values, drawing on your strengths and acting in line with what matters to you (your purpose), you will experience a more positively minded leadership. You will be better informed to make deliberate choices, and to notice what you are spending your time on and how that supports your purpose. By adopting the self-coaching strategies presented in the chapter, you will become more hopeful, energised, optimistic and confident. Your wellbeing is likely to increase as you lead as your best self.

Practices 2 and 3 will direct you to consider where you are heading in this ever-changing world. What *goals* would you like to achieve, and why do they matter to you? How will you increase and sustain your *motivation* to complete them and lead yourself towards success? How can you shape your goals so that they match your values and purpose and become meaningful to you?

Practice 4 supports you to build *self-awareness* and seek feedback. The intention here is to deepen your understanding of your behaviours, emotions and thoughts so you can lead your way through the transitions you experience. I'll help you identify the assumptions and beliefs you hold and suggest coaching strategies to monitor them.

Practices 5 and 6 consider how you manage your *time* and *energy*. Both of these go to the heart of how you lead yourself and the impact that results.

Practice 7 introduces the concept of your *personal board of directors* – your support crew. Who will you surround yourself with to support you in being your best self? Who will you engage as your advocates, mentors, coaches and reciprocal mentors?

The final five practices support how you lead others.

Practice 8 focuses on *exploring your leadership impact.* Using a number of different lenses, we will sharpen your focus on your visibility, trust, perceptions and behaviours as you explore your leadership shadow.

Practice 9 will assist you in *empowering* and delegating to others. We will focus on how you enable others and build their self-determination by considering how you are impacting their autonomy, competencies and sense of relatedness. How can you help your people feel that they matter and are engaged, empowered and entrusted?

Practices 10 and 11 tackle how you *listen* and *consciously communicate* with others. What is the impact of your communication? How can you become more in tune with how efficient, engaging and respectful you are?

Practice 12 will help you create a psychologically safe and *kind* space for those you lead. We will unravel how to create an environment that allows for diversity, inclusion, growth and engagement. This is essential for establishing your enduring leadership impact and ensuring people feel that they are of value.

Once you have worked through each chapter and begun applying the 12 practices, you will be better able to reflect on and influence the impact of your presence on others. You'll notice that you are inspiring, motivating, engaging and supporting others through your leadership. That is the leadership impact most people aim for. It allows others around you to feel they too can be their authentic selves, bringing their diverse backgrounds, points of view, cultures and ways of seeing the world to work. It's where your people feel encouraged and supported by you as they strive to fulfil their hopes and dreams, their goals and learnings. They feel safe and supported, that they are significant and that they matter.

Your experience of leadership is also bound to improve. You will find yourself more fulfilled and better able to share your journey with others in a positive way. Your leadership presence will continue in your absence and better the lives of those you engage with.

It's time to start self-coaching!

Practice 1

Leading as you

Arrie respected and enjoyed working with Dave. Dave was dynamic and inspiring and had built his followership by focusing on all things innovation. He was creative and a risk-taker, and as a result he engaged in what looked like exciting yet challenging projects. Dave had built his brand over many years. Arrie was motivated to be 'just like Dave'.

'What does that mean?' I asked in our coaching session. Arrie went on to describe Dave's personality, working style, strengths, clients and more, and reiterated what an awesome leader Dave was.

Yet Arrie struggled to enjoy his leadership role. To him, leadership felt awkward and had a sense of pretence. Leadership was a persona, which Arrie perpetuated during working hours. It took a lot of energy to act like Dave, sound like Dave and try to think like Dave. And although Dave appeared to have much success, Arrie did not feel he reached the same heights.

Arrie and I discussed an alternative stance. 'What if you could lead just like *you*? Lead as your best self?' I asked.

Arrie was curious and intrigued, and keen to explore what this could look like.

Leadership is complex, and more so when you don't have a great sense of self. Leading just like you requires you to initially engage with yourself to understand who you are as a leader. This allows you to lead more authentically. Rather than trying to be just like Dave, or any other impressive leader, you can be just like yourself: your *authentic* self.

Leading as you liberates you. It releases you from the pressure of trying to emulate someone else. After all, we are all diverse human beings, with different ways of communicating, different perspectives and different views of the world and its complex problems. We have different values, motives and preferences. We are challenged and excited by different pursuits and adopt different ways of leading. Yes, there may be some similarities between yourself and other leaders, but it is simply impossible to be identical to others. There are just too many variables and moving parts that distinguish us from each other.

Leading just like you consumes less energy. It takes less effort to be yourself than it does to try to be someone else. It's also fascinating and affirming to discover more about yourself and draw on those attributes and strengths to support you in your leadership, rather than mimicking someone else's style and approach. It builds your confidence as you become more at ease and accepting of who you are and what you can bring to your leadership.

Seeing your strengths and attributes with clear eyes will support you in being the leader you wish to be. You'll have a clear vision of the things that support and enable you. You'll see what excites and orientates you. You'll be more self-directed and alive to what will bring you pleasure in your work. And with those insights, your experience of leadership will be more positive and impactful.

Once I explained the benefits of leading with authenticity, Arrie agreed to focus on leading just like Arrie – rather than just like Dave. We agreed to a coaching approach that would support Arrie in self-discovery, enabling Arrie to explore what leading as his authentic self might look like. We started by exploring three areas, which I will now share with you as self-coaching strategies to add to your virtual backpack. They are: values, strengths and purpose.

Your values

Throughout your leadership journey it is important to be attuned to the values you wish to honour. Values are the principles that guide you in living your life. They provide you with a frame of beliefs to assist you with your decision-making.

Understanding which values are important to you provides a central premise for you to calibrate against in relation to your behaviours, emotions and thoughts. The more you mindfully connect with who you are and what you stand for, the easier it is to lead as yourself. The more in sync you are with your values, the easier it is to thread them through your life to support your leadership decisions and actions.

My values are very much shaped by my parents, who have strong values themselves. My parents were actively involved in the anti-apartheid movement in South Africa in the 1960s (in the days of Nelson Mandela and Joe Slovo). As a result of the values-based choices they made they had to flee South Africa avoiding arrest, only to discover they were then banned from returning for 30 years. My Mum is a descendant of those impacted by the Holocaust. Both of her parents escaped the most tragic events of that time, yet not without losing multitudes of family members and friends to the death camps. This certainly shaped her values, and mine.

The values my parents instilled in me were those of humanity, compassion, equity, respect and attention to assumptions and biases. They taught me about curiosity, kindness and the strength of family. I have tried to live my life by these values and lead through my professional career with them in mind. These are the beliefs that centre me in the leadership decisions I make. I haven't always got this right; for example, sometimes I've been overcommitted with work, yet other times I've managed to integrate work and family time more effortlessly and mindfully. Because I know family is one of my values, this gives me a compass to guide my decisions and a touchstone to assess my choices against.

I'm always interested to learn which values my coachees wish to honour, as it provides us with a basis for reflection in our coaching conversations. As you step forward with a focus on leading as you, the first thing to consider is which of *your* values you wish to honour in your leadership.

Take some time now to think about the values or beliefs that are meaningful to you. You might want to reflect on your life experiences and what has shaped you. What do you feel strongly about? What shapes your decision-making? What do you feel as truth deep in your core? What informs you as to what is right and wrong? What is meaningful to you in how you live your life and how you show up as you lead? These are the values that guide you.

Self-coaching exercise

Use Table 1 as a prompt to identify your key values. Circle your top five or add additional values to those listed, and then write them in your notebook so you can be mindful of the values that will shape you as you lead your way.

Knowing what you value at your core will assist you in leading as you. The more you are conscious of your belief structure, the easier it will be for you to shape your leadership decisions with these beliefs in mind. The practice of leading as you encourages increased connection with your values, which in turn increases your self-belief and self-assurance. You become more aware of who you are and what you stand for and are able to reflect this through your leadership actions, inspiring and motivating others around you. It also creates a more sustainable leadership model for you to enact. You represent yourself as you.

Be active in becoming more conscious of your values. Write your values on a sticky note and pin this to your desk, notice board, bathroom mirror or another other chosen space where you can read them daily. Hold your values close to the surface of your mind as you lead your way. In a short while you'll be amazed at how positively minded you feel as you connect with your values and lead as your best self.

Table 1: Values

Abundance	Achievement	Adventure
Affiliation	Altruism	Authenticity
Care	Challenge	Collaboration
Commitment	Community	Compassion
Connection	Control	Cooperation
Courage	Creativity	Curiosity
Discipline	Diversity	Drama
Empathy	Engagement	Environmental conservation
Equality	Equity	Fairness
Family	Financial wellbeing	Flexibility
Forgiveness	Friendship	Fulfilment
Fun	Generosity	Grace
Gratitude	Happiness	Harmony
Health	Honesty	Hope
Humanity	Independence	Individuality
Influence	Integrity	Kindness
Leadership	Learning	Love
Mattering	Meaning	Musicality
Optimism	Passion	Politics
Power	Presence	Purpose
Recognition	Respect	Security
Service	Sharing	Spirituality
Spontaneity	Support	Tradition
Trust	Wisdom	Wonder

Your strengths

Strengths differ to values. Strengths are the things that feel effortless. They energise you and allow you to be at your best. When you are working to your strengths as your best self, you are more positively minded and resilient, and more open to possibilities. Your wellbeing improves. You are better able to solve complex problems and inspire, motivate and engage with yourself and others. You are better placed to lead as you – to lead with confidence and as your best self.

I love to encourage my coachees to draw upon their strengths to build their confidence. Typically my coachees are quick to tell me what they are *not* good at. However, once you focus on what strengthens you, on what supports you when you are at your best, you'll have a better understanding of yourself and draw positive energy from utilising your strengths.

When you recognise your strengths, you will increase your capacity to face differing situations. You can dial your strengths up or down when appropriate to support yourself. The first step is to establish what your key strengths are.

Self-coaching exercise

In your notebook, fill in the columns in Table 2. Be generous with yourself. Fill the page with as many examples as possible. This is your truth!

What you have listed represents you at your best – your expertise, your key experiences and your best interactions and relationships. Reflecting on this, identify your key strengths, which should now be apparent. Complete your own version of the example in Table 3 in your notebook. This reflects your key strengths that come to mind when you are at your best. You can use the table of strengths (Table 4 overleaf) to help you identify your corresponding strengths.

Table 2: My expertise and powers

What is my expertise?	What are my experiential powers?	What are my social powers?
List all of your qualifications, diplomas, degrees, courses and key certificates.	List the experiences that represent you at your best (for instance, promotions, particular roles you have fulfilled, winning proposals, great presentations, awesome reports you've written, successful negotiations, times you have delivered tough feedback, complex problems you have solved, successful teams you have built and so on).	List the interactions and responsibilities that represent you as your best social self (for instance, you're a great parent, fun partner, kind friend, volunteer, sportsperson, artist, singer, community member and so on).

Table 3: My strengths – example

My strengths	Examples of when my strengths arise
Sound judgement	This arises during key negotiations and interactions with my stakeholders. It has helped me position myself for opportunities.
Driven	I am able to achieve goals, as represented by the completion of my masters degree.
Kindness	My kindness comes through in setting kind business objectives, and also being available to help family and friends in need.
Rapport-builder	I quickly build rapport with those I coach, both in a professional and voluntary capacity, which supports relationship formation.
Organised	My organisational skills have supported me with my many roles and goals.

Table 4: Strengths

Able to see the big picture	Accountable	Adaptable
Agile	Approachable	Cautious
Coach	Collaborative	Commercially minded
Compassionate	Competitive	Considered
Courageous	Culturally aware	Curious
Decisive	Detail-oriented	Diligent
Driven	Effective communicator	Empathic
Enabler	Energetic	Generous
Good memory	Heavy lifter	Honest
Hopeful	Humorous	Ideator
Inclusive	Influencer	Innovative
Inquisitive	Inspirational	Instinctive
Intellectually astute	Intuitive	Kind
Listener	Market-maker	Mentally tough
Mentor	Motivator	Narrator
Observant	Optimistic	Organised
Patient	Persuasive	Planful
Pragmatic	Proactive	Problem-solver
Rapport-builder	Relatable	Relationship-builder
Reliable	Resilient	Responsive
Risk-alert	Self-aware	Self-confident
Sociable	Sound judgement	Storyteller
Strong leader	Strong work ethic	Team-builder
Technically proficient	Trustworthy	Values-driven

Once you have completed this exercise, grab your phone and take a photo of the page in your notebook. Create an album in your photos app called 'me' and relocate the photo to this album. We are always on the go, so the likelihood of you finding this photo in the future will diminish unless you are deliberate about filing it. Having it located on your phone helps you access your view of you at your best, your list of strengths, as frequently as you need to boost your confidence and remind you of all the great things you have done and represent. This page of strengths is a factual representation of you as your best self. When you have a shaky crisis of confidence as a leader, use it to remind yourself of the person you are. You should be proud of what you have achieved and what you represent!

Your purpose

If you really want to take big strides as a leader you must consider and articulate your purpose. When you approach your leadership role knowing what is important to you, why you choose to do what you do, why you are significant and why you matter in doing what you do, you will increase meaning, self-efficacy, motivation and capacity for engagement. You will experience increased positive emotions such as hope, optimism and inspiration. You will be better placed to tackle the complex problems you exist to solve as you will be more open to possibilities.

In my experience, people find it quite challenging to define their purpose and why they matter. Not many of my coachees jump up and say, 'I've got this!' before rattling off their purpose. More often than not, coachees will skip over their *why* – their purpose – and talk instead about *what* they do. The *what* is important, but it has more impact if you can give it meaning – if you can lift it from the tactical, operational day-to-day to something more intrinsic and meaningful to you.

I take inspiration from the work of leadership expert Zach Mercurio, who helped me better understand how to determine my purpose. Mercurio speaks of identifying the world problem you exist to solve, which will help you determine why you matter.[4] He defines authentic purpose as your 'genuine and unique reason for existence that is useful to others in society'.[5] He further explains that when you believe you matter in fulfilling this reason for existence, you take responsibility for achieving the resulting impact on the world, and that's where your purpose lies.

When I thought about it from this perspective, I discovered I knew my purpose the whole time. I had been working towards fulfilling my purpose, yet I hadn't articulated it very well. As a result, my purpose sat well below the surface of my consciousness and I focused too much on ticking off my goals, rather than approaching my work in a meaningful way. Once I stopped to realise why I coach and why I matter, the way I led changed. Articulating my purpose helped me shape my goals to support me directionally towards what was most meaningful to me.

Using your systems mindset and following Mercurio's work, you can recognise that everything you do, every job you hold, every company that operates, every government that legislates is focused on solving human problems. Once you realise that you exist to solve a human problem, it becomes easier to articulate your purpose – why the work you do, the leadership you bring, is of significance and matters. Your 'mattering' is connected to your purpose.[6] You can then curate your goals to reflect the importance of the problem you are trying to solve.

For example, my problem statement sounds something like this: 'Globally we experience inequity in the designation of male and female corporate leaders. Women's participation in corporate decision-making is not on par with their male counterparts.'

My leadership coaching supports women's full and effective participation in corporate leadership. It encourages equitable opportunities for leadership at all levels of decision-making in political, social, economic and public life. My coaching work supports the creation of improved work practices and helps develop kind leaders who create opportunities *for all*. The ripple effect of this makes the world a better place. This is why I matter. This is my purpose. I am significant in fulfilling this given my leadership and coaching expertise; I can bring unique insights and perspective, be empathic and compassionate, and act in support of others towards resolving this human problem.

Let's play with some more examples to further illustrate purpose.

It may be that your job is to lead a consumer business organisation. You are ensuring the creation of goods for consumption by the community. You are fulfilling a demand for a human need, whether that be food, cleaning products, packaging products or other consumer goods. Your organisation is helping the community live a better life through access to quality, safe and reliable goods, and is improving people's wellbeing. This is the human problem you are solving. You are significant in solving this human problem given your understanding of the industry, your strategic thinking, your support of research and development and your leadership skills. This is why you matter.

Perhaps you lead a financial services organisation. You are ensuring the community's financial wellbeing through the safe and effective distribution of funds, allowing for a functioning economy, which provides financial stability and wellbeing. This is the human problem you are solving. You are significant given your financial background, your deep understanding of global financial instruments, your ability to solve complex problems and your leadership skills. That is why you matter.

Self-coaching exercise

Ask yourself the following three questions, as Mercurio suggests, to determine your purpose:

1. What is the human problem that exists that you are here to solve?
2. Why are you significant in solving this human problem?
3. Why do you matter?[7]

You have just described your purpose. Write it down in your notebook.

Now that you know your purpose – the particular direction in which you are headed and why it is meaningful to you – your focus will be sharpened. You will use your precious time more effectively, devoting more energy to the things that matter and less to the things that don't. You will build your confidence by understanding the reasons you're doing what you plan to do.

If you know your purpose you can share why your goals are meaningful and impactful, which is likely to inspire others and create a deeper understanding of why you lead your way. It will assist you in leading others, providing a navigational focus that others may be inspired by and motivated to work towards with you.

Your leadership shadow

All leaders cast a leadership shadow. Your shadow is a reflection of how you act, what you represent and what you role model. It's what people around you notice of you, and it can affect them positively or negatively. Your leadership shadow reflects your leadership intention. It is shaped by your values, strengths and purpose and how you bring all of them together in your behaviours, emotions and thoughts.

Now that you have a clearer understanding of what you stand for, the strengths you can draw upon to be your best self, and what matters to you, you can be more conscious of the shadow you cast. You can role model what it means to lead as you and positively influence, inspire and motivate with this in mind.

You can set the stage. You can demonstrate what it means to lead with authenticity, making values-based decisions and setting purpose-based goals. You can become more deliberate in how you lead. You can lead with greater consistency as you now better understand the basis from which you lead. Better still, you can lead with more confidence and as you lead as *you* – as your best self.

Self-coaching summary

♦ Leading as you allows you to lead with your values in mind, towards what matters most to you, using your strengths to support you.

♦ It's *your* leadership journey. Empower yourself to make choices about where you are headed and why. You can lead *your* way.

♦ Recognising what matters to you and why gives you meaning and can support you in selecting meaningful, purposeful and fulfilling goals.

♦ Once you understand your purpose you can mindfully cast your leadership shadow and positively influence, inspire and motivate others as you lead as your best self.

Practice 2

Setting your goals

'Stretched. Yep, that's how I'd frame it,' said Jos. 'I've got so many things on my to-do list. I feel like I'm being pulled in too many directions.'

Jos was a driven and highly capable leader who was willing to get involved in the many initiatives presented to her. In fact, she was often *too* willing. As a result she would find herself with a long list of things to do, often representing others' priorities rather than her own.

She enjoyed being challenged and recognised for her achievements, and had for a time been pretty good at coordinating herself to get things done. But lately Jos had felt concerned about where this was taking her. She liked the variety of projects she was involved in but worried that she was filling her days with 'stuff' – and often not *her* stuff. She couldn't articulate what her focus was, nor how she could make an impact as a leader. She guessed that her impact would reflect someone who was dependable and supportive of others. Yet this was not the full story of how she wanted to be known.

Jos and I spent some time exploring this, which led us to a goal-focused discussion. Without her own well-articulated goals, Jos had found herself floating between other people's goals. These goals were interesting, yet they didn't make her feel that she was being a true leader or driving initiatives that mattered.

Jos was being reactive to opportunities around her, rather than strategic in how she advanced as a leader. She hadn't invested in self-coaching. She was *doing* leadership, rather than *being* a leader. She wanted to unpack how she could design and articulate her own goals to provide her with focus, meaning and fulfilment as a leader. As Jos realised, self-coaching to design your own goals enables you to lead with purpose. You will be more effective in how you use your time, what you pay attention to and the impact you have.

Some people fear that creating goals creates too much commitment. If this is your view, you may have thoughts such as 'I'm not sure what I want to do,' or 'I like to take things as they come.' This is a perfect prompt to start crafting goals reflecting *why* you want to do what you do, and then assess what you want to do and how you can achieve it. Pausing to craft purposeful goals that will have a desired impact that *matters to you* is essential in leading a purposeful life.

Given that you are leading yourself, you can redesign your goals whenever you believe it's appropriate. You can assess whether the choices you are making and the direction you are heading in are supporting you to find meaning and fulfilment.

Additionally, where you lead others, you can bring your purpose and goals to life, inspiring your team members so they understand the destination and how they can be involved. You can be impactful as you lead your way.

Let's examine some self-coaching strategies for setting your goals.

How to set your goals

People tend to be goal-directed beings with a general understanding of where they are going and why they want to get there. Creating a *meaningful goal narrative* forges a stronger connection with your goals and reduces your chances of being pulled off course by other competing priorities. This narrative should reflect what matters most to you and the impact you would like to have – your *why*. Crystallising your goals removes the surrounding fogginess. You take control of where you are headed, rather than blindly arriving at a destination (if you arrive at all!).

Most leaders I coach are goal-oriented. They are at their best when they understand their purpose and have identified exactly how to enact it. When working with my coachees on goal setting, I like to ask, 'What might success look like in 12 months' time? What impact you would like to have?' Asking this of yourself will help you pinpoint your destination, and from there you can start to unpack your related goals – the road map to get you there.

Self-coaching exercise

In Practice 1 you considered what gives you meaning, fulfilment and purpose in your professional life. It will be helpful having this information front and centre as you discover how to incorporate your *why* and create goals that detail your *what* and *how*.

To create your meaningful goal narrative, respond to the following questions in your notebook:

1. Articulate your *why*. What matters to you? What leadership impact would you like to have? Why is this important to you? (For example, *I am passionate about bringing equity to coaching by making self-coaching skills more accessible to a greater number of leaders. I feel strongly that I can increase access to coaching support by bringing my coaching expertise forward rather than watching from the sidelines. This matters to me as I can play a small part in helping others better themselves and their impact on others. This will improve the wellbeing of people, organisations and communities and, in a small way, make this world a better place.*)

2. Considering your *why*, what does success look like to you in 12 months' time? (*In 12 months' time success looks like a greater number of leaders using self-coaching practices to improve their leadership impact and lead as their best selves.*)

3. What is required for you to achieve this impact? *(For this to be true, I need to set my personal goal to activate my book and deliver 12 self-coaching practices to as many leaders as possible.)*

You now have the basis of *why* you need to set your goals and what success could look like, and can continue to build your goals from here.

Your *why* is the best place to start with goal setting, yet it needs the *what* and the *how* to become a goal that can be executed. As you articulate your goals you can reflect on all three facets. I consider your *why* to be the most powerful part of your goals as it will drive and motivate you, so I suggest you thread it through your goals by using value-based goal statements.

Value-based goals

Value-based goals align with your beliefs and preferences. They represent your true north. You can assess them against your internal compass to determine whether you are heading in a direction that aligns with what you regard as important, what is meaningful to you and what corresponds with your belief system. When your goals resonate with your true north, you are more likely to put in sustained effort towards the completion of the goal, increasing your goal satisfaction and personal wellbeing. This makes it much easier for you to lead your way.

You can draw upon the values you identified in Practice 1 to assist you in designing and shaping your goals. For instance, if you strongly value kindness, you might set goals that incorporate building kindness into your leadership style and your business objectives. You might focus on goals around corporate responsibility such as equality and inclusion within your workplace or team.

If you value being competitive and driven, you might shape goals that stretch your personal targets to incentivise you to drive growth further and be a market leader.

If you value reliability and resourcefulness, your goals could reflect these attributes – such as solving a particularly complex problem, or reliably showing up in meetings in support of your team members.

If, like me, you value family, you might build some mechanisms into your goals to support you in spending time with your family while also meeting your priorities at work. For example, your goals might be around building a high-performing team that allows for empowerment and delegation of projects and tasks, resulting in you having additional time for your family. Or perhaps your goals might consider how and where you perform your work, to lessen your travel schedule and enable you to have more flexibility to spend time with your family.

Whatever your values, with a little bit of foresight you should be able to consciously incorporate them into your leadership goals. Threading your values and purpose through your goals ensures you are leading your way towards a meaningful and fulfilling life.

Using a goal hierarchy

Utilising a goal hierarchy is a great way to create a comprehensive roadmap to guide your way.[8] A goal hierarchy categorises your goals according to their time span. Once you identify a longer-term goal you can then craft shorter-term goals to support it (see Figure 3).

Figure 3: Goal hierarchy

From an organisational point of view, contemplating goals over 12 months can be beneficial, particularly as organisations tend to assess employee performance from year to year. Consider your longer-term goal as a goal you are hopeful to attain within 12 to 24 months. This might be an aspirational goal, and should represent your vision and what matters to you, and be aligned with your purpose and values.

The shorter-term goals should be attained within a selected period. It's important to give equal attention to each of your shorter-term goals. If all of your efforts are spent on one or two of the shorter-term goals, you may experience goal neglect in relation to the remaining goals.[9] If one or more of the shorter-term goals is not attained, the likelihood of reaching the longer-term goal is diminished. Think of it like a mathematical equation:

Longer-term goal = Shorter-term goal 1 + shorter-term goal 2 + shorter-term goal 3 + shorter-term goal 4 + …

For instance, imagine your longer-term goal is to be promoted to General Manager in 12 months. To attain this goal, you have identified the following shorter-term goals:

1. Develop your team's skills and capacity so that you can step up to operate as a General Manager.
2. Further develop your delegation skills.
3. Further develop your strategic management skills.
4. Build deeper relationships with your senior stakeholders.

If you focus only on two or three of these goals, it is likely that you will not achieve the longer-term goal, as it depends on your attainment of each of the shorter-term goals. Neglecting to develop your delegation skills may lead to an unintended increase in your workload. This may distort the evidence of your leadership capability, as you may be perceived as a team member who is skilled at *delivering* work, rather than leading and *delegating* work effectively. Your increased workload might also limit the time you have to invest in achieving your other shorter-term goals. You might not have thought about this consequence when you neglected to focus on developing your delegation skills, yet the impact of your actions, or inactions, may impede your ability to achieve your longer-term goal.

Bringing your goals to life

Describing your goals is the first step, but bringing them to life – doing the work necessary to achieve them – is equally important. I work with many clients who love setting goals but find orienting themselves to their achievement challenging.

Adam was a positively minded man who arrived at our first meeting with a great deal of enthusiasm for his goals. He oozed excitement as he recounted what he had in mind in creating his business. Each time we met, he relished telling me what his goal was and how fabulous it was going to be when he achieved it. He could picture the outcome and the success it would bring. He could visualise how he would feel on its completion and was very motivated towards its success.

Adam was working with me because he found bringing his goal to life a challenge. He had excellent goal orientation but lacked the discipline to complete the work required. I encouraged Adam to think of his goals using a travel metaphor. He realised there was no point investing time looking through travel websites to see where he would go if he wasn't actually getting in the car and commencing his journey. His journey had failed to progress. When he had started working towards his goals, he found himself stalling repeatedly. He could still visualise what he wanted, yet couldn't establish how to get there.

Adam used the SMART goals tool, which you may already be familiar with, to bring his goals to life. Setting SMART goals increases your likelihood of pursuing *and* attaining them.[10]

SMART goals are those defined as:

- **S**pecific
- **M**easurable
- **A**ttainable
- **R**elevant
- **T**ime-based.

Let's take a look at each of these aspects.

Specific

Clarify your goals by making them specific. This ensures that the goal can be readily understood as you make progress. It helps you understand exactly what you need to do. You are more likely to complete goal-directed activities if you can easily understand the specifics of your goal, rather than reflecting on the goal in broad, ambiguous and general terms. Specific goals help you uncover the route you need to take for their completion and point to the way in which you will reach a tangible outcome.

A specific leadership-related goal may sound like:

I aim to build my understanding of psychological safety so I can lead teams in which people feel safe to participate and are free of the risk of embarrassment or humiliation. I plan to learn how to invite team members to participate and offer their point of view so they feel included as part of the team.

A less specific goal may sound like:

I plan to build my understanding of psychological safety.

To ensure the goal is sufficiently specific, consider:

- What is required to attain the goal?
- What are the boundaries of this goal?
- What's inside and what's outside of this goal?

Measurable

Adding some measurements to the goal will help you track your progress and determine when you have achieved it. It gives you milestones to work towards and, going back to the travel metaphor, will help you determine whether your journey has been worthwhile.

Be careful not to create measurements that are difficult to assess. For example, if your goal is to make a meaningful impact in the industry you work in, how would you measure a 'meaningful impact'? Is it too subjective or vague in its measure, leaving you and others questioning how to progress towards the completion of the goal?

I like to test my goal statement and its measure, and how others would interpret them, to ensure they can be objectively understood.

Attainable

Your goals should be attainable: possible to achieve and realistic. I discourage you from setting a goal or measure that 'knocks you out of the park'. In other words, don't set a goal that seems almost impossible to attain, as your level of motivation towards completing it is likely to diminish once you recognise the impossibility.

For instance, if your goal involves growing your revenue by 15 per cent per annum, this may be a significant stretch target that is perceived as unattainable within the current economic climate. If you believe there is limited chance of success you will be unlikely to pursue the goal with much vigour.

Reviewing your goal's attainability also helps you identify any obstacles you might encounter as you progress towards your desired outcome. It gives you foresight to consider how to navigate around or through such circumstances. This may include identifying support or resources you might require to attain the goal.

For instance, to attain your goal of promotion to the Business Unit Leadership Team within the next 12 months, you may require your leader's support in allocating additional resources (a team) so that you can practise your empowerment and strategic management skills.

Relevant

Relevance considers whether the goal makes sense in relation to what you are hoping to achieve. Think of it as the litmus test. Does each shorter-term goal support the attainment of the longer-term goal? Why is this goal important and how is it relevant?

Sometimes we construct goals that actually divert our attention away from where we are headed. The goal in isolation may be interesting and exciting, however it might not be relevant to the larger plan. For instance, if one of my goals was to build my professional skills in an adjacent industry, this on its own might be a reasonable and worthwhile professional goal. However, it might not be appropriate to prioritise when I consider how it relates to achieving my longer-term goal.

Time-based

Goals can be isolated into time-based blocks, helping to create expectations of when particular activities are to occur on the pathway to reach the longer-term goal.

Dividing a goal into smaller, incremental goals to be achieved within particular time frames can be more motivating than simply working towards a bigger goal. Each time a smaller goal is achieved you are able to note its success, which motivates you to continue. This structured approach to goal setting can help to sustain your pathway towards the longer-term goal. It also helps in making the goal attainable, as you can organise your time against each goal – a bit like establishing which part of a journey you will complete over a span of time, such as a few hours, a day, a week or a month.

Breaking your goals down

Returning to our goal equation, think about how you can break your goals down into smaller incremental parts:

Longer-term goal = sum of shorter-term goals
Shorter-term goals = sum of each goal's constituent parts

Identifying the constituent parts of each shorter-term goal allows you to break down these goals into smaller, achievable sub-goals to be completed in relevant time frames. This makes it easier to get your head around what needs to be done, moving you towards key tasks. It also helps you to build confidence, as small wins resulting from the completion of incremental goals supports your positive mindset and builds hope.

Learning goals

Learning goals, sometimes called mastery goals, focus on *performing* the tasks related to the goal, and on the learning that eventuates – rather than on the goal outcome. Setting these types of goals helps you build your mastery and improve your performance and growth, making them highly suitable for leadership-related goals. They also better support you in working towards the things that matter most to you – your *why* – as they allow you to learn along the way and feel more fulfilled in satisfying your goals. They are more likely to result in higher job satisfaction, organisational commitment and work engagement without increasing the risk of burnout.

Learning goals help you build your skills and understanding, creating greater confidence and self-belief and improved performance.[11] Adopting learning goals makes you better able to deal with poor performance or failure and bounce back from setbacks faster than if you had set performance-based goals. When you set learning goals, poor performance is viewed as a learning experience rather than a negative event.[12]

So, what might a learning goal look like? Let's take a look at an example. Imagine you have set yourself the following goal:

To lead a high-performing team.

When the goal is expressed in this way, it's difficult to identify the competencies you intend to develop in yourself to reach the goal.

Let's reframe the goal as a learning goal:

To develop my strategic and agile thinking skills to enable me to better lead a high-performing team.

Your professional development and growth is now an integral part of the goal. This development will eventuate through developing further leadership competencies. You are hoping to use these skills to lead a high-performing team, which will set your focus on how you will perform with these newly acquired skills.

The more you turn your attention to learning, the greater your opportunity to develop. Your learnings might focus on a new technical skill or method. Your technical learnings compound as you progress, supporting you to achieve your goals.

Your learning goals may also include professional skills such as empathy and listening. You might set a learning goal such as:

To mindfully listen to my colleagues, I need to activate my curiosity rather than impatiently jump to conclusions.

Achieving this goal will require you to master mindful, active listening skills, and use inquiry and questioning skills to satisfy your curiosity regarding others' contributions. Your learnings will provide you with further insights to test your assumptions, and will help you demonstrate your skills of inclusivity through hearing others' diverse views. Your new skills will also allow the people around you to feel heard. (You can read more about developing your active listening skills in Practice 10.)

Your learnings should also relate to your broader capabilities and how they help you attain your goals. The following questions will help you build your self-awareness and effectiveness, supporting you to learn more about your leadership as you lead your way:

- In what ways do you support yourself or get in your own way of achieving your goals? (For example, 'I tend to work independently yet am open to seeking insights from others when advancing my goals.')

- What patterns are you noticing in your behaviours, emotions and thoughts, and how are these assisting you with achieving your goals? (For example, 'When I am excited about my goals, I tend to jump in quickly to advance them without paying mindful attention to my goal strategies. This can lead to inefficiencies in how I use my time and increase my stress as deadlines approach.')

- What might you learn about the assumptions you hold, the character traits you have, the judgements you carry and the factors that motivate you? (For example, 'I have become better at testing my assumptions to ensure that they are true. I am working on noticing the biases I carry that shape my thinking and impact my levels of motivation towards goal completion.')

- What might you learn about how and when you perform at your best, and which strengths you draw upon to do so? (For example, 'I perform at my best when I have planned my approach towards my goal achievement and utilise my strengths of love of learning, planfulness and communication.')

- What might you learn about the way you see the world and how it influences your behaviours, emotions and thoughts? (For example, 'I have an optimistic and trusting view of others while also working with a level of healthy scepticism. I am curious about other people's ideas and thought processes. This helps me find solutions to problems I encounter.')

The more that you can build your self-awareness, the more you will be able to make choices that support you in attaining your goals. (We'll discuss self-awareness in more detail in Practice 4).

Self-coaching exercise

- Use the goal hierarchy to craft your longer- and shorter-term goals.
- Check whether each of your goals is SMART and refine as required.
- Reflect on your values and purpose (your *why*, as you identified in Practice 1) in developing your longer-term goal.
- When shaping your shorter-term goals, consider what needs to be true to support your attainment of your longer-term goal.
- Create learning goals to ensure meaningful and fulfilling outcomes.
- Ask yourself the key learning questions to increase your mindfulness and self-awareness.

Self-coaching summary

- Goal-directed behaviour ensures impact as you lead your way.
- Align your goals with your values and purpose to make them more meaningful.
- Plan your goals and revise them annually.
- A goal hierarchy can assist you with identifying longer-term goals and supporting shorter-term goals.
- Make each goal SMART.
- Ensure the sum of the shorter-term goals leads to fulfilment of the longer-term goal.
- Learning or mastery goals are most likely to result in higher job satisfaction, organisational commitment and work engagement without increasing the risk of burnout.

Practice 3

Being motivated

'Guess what I have to do?' said Ethan. 'My director has assigned the redesign of our department to me. I've got to reshape it to incorporate an adjacent department and then lead the new team and increase revenue by 5 per cent. This will be hard work.'

Ethan had a clear goal in front of him. It was a goal he felt he *had* to take on. Although it was unanticipated, he knew why he was selected for the task. He knew he had a reputation for successfully dealing with complex restructures. He was well regarded by his leadership team and able to attain challenging goals. He understood the scope, the time frame and what had to be done, and had been empowered to act – yet his level of motivation towards the goal was low. The goal would redirect his attention away from what he had hoped to focus on that year, which was building his eminence as an industry leader. His lack of motivation was affecting his demeanour, and he'd had feedback that this was rippling out to his team. Not only was he feeling demotivated, but he realised he was having a negative impact on those around him. His leadership impact was diminishing.

Ethan wanted to explore how he could lead effectively towards the successful achievement of this goal. What could he do to become engaged, inspired and motivated towards the goal? How could he be impactful in leading and fulfilling this goal? This conversation presented an opportunity to focus on goal motivation. Ethan and I had previously invested time discussing why and how he should set his goals to enable him to lead his way (very much like what we discussed in Practice 2). However, as I explained to Ethan, setting goals is just the start. Finding the motivation to pursue your goals is essential for goal fulfilment.

As you lead your way, you're highly likely to experience swings in your level of motivation. At times you may feel energised and lead yourself in an effortless way; but it's also possible to find yourself demotivated and challenged to progress with your goals.

Being motivated towards your goals helps you achieve them. When you are lacking motivation, you are less likely to have the desire to achieve your goals, which can affect your leadership impact. Becoming motivated is helpful in leaning into the challenges ahead of you, becoming positively minded and open to possibility so you can shape change.

Mindset and motivation

Motivation can be considered on a spectrum, from external (controlled) motivation to intrinsic (autonomous) motivation (see Figure 4).[13] The greater your level of intrinsic motivation, the greater your alignment with your values, and the greater your motivation to pursue your goals.

Figure 4: The motivation spectrum

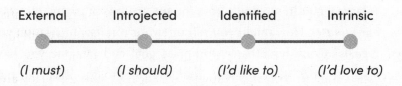

ADAPTED FROM RM RYAN AND EL DECI, 'SELF-DETERMINATION THEORY AND THE FACILITATION OF INTRINSIC MOTIVATION, SOCIAL DEVELOPMENT, AND WELL-BEING', *AMERICAN PSYCHOLOGIST*, 2000, 55(1):68–78.

As leaders we're often faced with external goals that we must motivate ourselves to achieve. For example, we may have key performance indicators (KPIs), which are commonly set by others. Your senior leaders may determine that a part of your goal is to meet a particular financial target, improve growth or revenue by X per cent, increase headcount by Y per cent, integrate one business into another (as in Ethan's case), or other, similar targets. These goals tend to have an external (controlled) motivating factor affixed to them, where you are advised that you *must* achieve the goal in question. The goals tend to lack much room for you to personally shape and determine them and are often created without considerable consultation with you. The challenge in such cases (and as faced by Ethan) is to determine how to best engage with these external motivations and pursue the goal.

Referencing your values may provide you with a tool to shift your level of motivation and engagement with the goal, making it easier to lead your way. If you can align the goal more closely with your values, it moves from being external to you, where you feel you *must* pursue the goal, to introjected, where you feel you *should* pursue the goal.

Better yet is when your motivation moves further across the spectrum from feeling you *should* progress the goal to where you would *like* to pursue the goal. This stance is where your motivation is identified, and your behaviours are regulated by personal values attached to the task. You feel more autonomous.

The most desired position is where you would simply love to pursue the goal. In such cases, you are acting in alignment with your values and are intrinsically motivated to pursue the goal. Your behaviours are integrated with your values and beliefs at this point.

A large factor in moving across the spectrum is in paying *attention to your mindset*. How might you reframe your mindset in relation you your goals? Consider Ethan's workplace goal and imagine you have been set this goal by your leader. You have been told to lead your new team to increase your business revenue by 5 per cent over the next year. This goal is externally motivated: you have been advised what you *must* achieve to have success, and you may not feel highly attached to or motivated by this goal. Such a goal can be challenging to lead through.[14] To increase your level of motivation you can try to align the goal with your values. By altering your mindset (the way you consider the goal), you may be able to move it from something you *must* do to something you *should* do. For example, if you value supporting other team members' success, you might reframe the goal noting that you *should* lead your team towards this outcome as it will provide more opportunities for their growth and development. By increasing revenue by 5 per cent through selling more business products or services, you may be more likely to deliver further developmental opportunities for your team.

In time, you may be able to move your mindset from thinking of the goal as something you *should* do to something you would *like* to do. Perhaps you value respect and collaboration and you would like to increase revenue by 5 per cent, as doing so will allow you to also build deeper relationships with your clients and collaborate with them in solving their complex problems. This may be a meaningful way to apply your leadership skills – something that is more aligned with your values. Who knows, you may even end up *loving* the goal, which is where you feel intrinsically motivated by the goal and it is integrated with your core beliefs and values.

Goals that align with your personal values are self-concordant goals.[15] Pursuing such goals has been shown to increase your well-being; from a holistic point of view, it provides you with a better quality of life, and it is a preferred state for a leader.[16] If you design your professional goals to be self-concordant, you are better able to positively impact your happiness and likelihood of pursuing the goals, striving towards a meaningful outcome.

Self-determination

Self-determination is an important factor in improving your motivation towards your goals and developing optimism, confidence and resilience. Self-determination is a psychological theory that considers your inherent motivation.[17] The theory suggests that people who are high in self-determination will have increased self-belief and self-confidence. This creates more positive emotions and feelings of hope and optimism, which contribute to your wellbeing. As your positive emotions and wellbeing increase, you are better able to develop solutions to complex problems. Your levels of hope and optimism increase your capacity to open your mind and broaden your pathway thinking, which should support you with your goal attainment.[18]

Self-determination theory encompasses three constructs – autonomy, competency and relatedness – which together support a person's need to become more motivated to grow. This motivation aids people in their adoption of behaviours, emotions and thoughts that may reflect optimism, confidence and resilience. Let's take a look at the three constructs in more detail.

Autonomy

Earlier in this chapter I mentioned that externally motivated goals can be difficult to action. By comparison, your ability to alter behaviours and maintain them for a longer period arises when you are autonomously motivated – when you are able to exercise your own choice or your own volition.

The more autonomous a person is regarding a given behaviour, the more effort, engagement, persistence and stability they are likely to express.[19] For example, as a coach my goal is to be best-in-service to my coachees, providing bespoke and impactful coaching support. I work autonomously, making choices concerning how and when I schedule coaching appointments. I design my working day with breaks between coaching conversations to allow for the completion of my coaching notes, resulting actions and administration. I carve out time for academic reading, coursework and coaching supervision to advance my technical skills. I include wellbeing breaks in my working day, allowing me to attend the next coaching session focused, recharged, fully present, attentive and engaged. The choices I make support my positive motivation towards my goal achievement.

So, how do you find autonomy when setting leadership goals at work? The more that you can *feel* like you have a choice in relation to your goals, the more autonomous you will be. This perception can drive the related behaviours. The basis of your autonomy may stem from pursuing a goal because of interest or enjoyment, because of the inherent importance of the goal or because the goal reflects your values.[20] This autonomy and empowerment allows for goal-directed, self-regulated behaviours and increases your ability to act of your own volition. Your motivation is improved.

Self-coaching exercise

Start with some simple self-reflective questions as a part of your self-coaching:

- How can I design the goal to increase my autonomy?
- What is in my control?
- What and whom can I influence in relation to this goal?
- What decisions can I make with regards to how I pursue the goal?
- How much control do I have over the time I spend on this goal?
- How can I act independently? Are there approval processes to be aware of?
- What information or support might I require to pursue the goal?
- What choices can I make in relation to the goal?

You can also, as best as you can, make choices regarding your behaviours, emotions and thoughts to increase your motivation. You can support your levels of goal confidence by:

- choosing to focus on what is in your control regarding your behaviours, emotions and thoughts
- determining what is realistic in setting and achieving goals

- assessing what increases your stores of emotional and physical energy
- identifying what gives you purpose and meaning in what you are doing.

Competency

When you are able to develop your competencies or apply your mastery, your self-belief and confidence increases, giving you a better chance of achieving your desired outcomes. You are also further motivated when you can demonstrate your own competencies. Just as a child enjoys being positively recognised for displaying their competencies, we adults too are motivated by our sense of fulfilment when displaying our mastery. Our sense of self-worth increases.

You should consider this when setting your goals, as your motivation is likely to increase as you apply and develop your level of competency. Research has found that:

> *Competence promotes the pursuit of challenging and deeply satisfying experiences and is a criterion for psychological growth and well-being... Rather than reflecting a static state of being competent or skilful at something, the need for competence is ongoing and promotes persistence and continued action.*[21]

This drives motivation and makes it easier to lead yourself.

Developing your technical capability through training, development and experiential learning will build your competency, self-belief and self-efficacy. Competencies can include technical skills, subject matter expertise, professional skills and 'people' skills.

Self-coaching exercise

When designing your goals, give some thought to how you will build your competencies. Reflect on the following five questions:

1. Which competencies are required to fulfil your goal?

2. How can you build your skills to increase your level of competency?

3. How can you demonstrate your skills through completing this goal?

4. Which additional adjacent skills or capabilities can be developed while completing this goal? This might include skills in problem-solving, communication, relationship-building, collaboration and teamwork or leadership, or technical skills such as strategic thinking, financial management or digital design.

5. How might you focus on the constituent parts of your competencies to further develop and demonstrate them? For instance, if you wanted to demonstrate your teamwork competencies, you might focus on your approach to collaboration, 'forming and norming' teams, conflict resolution, your ability to take on differing roles within a team, your approach to determining and delivering towards a common team purpose and your active inclusion of all team members within projects.

Relatedness

When you have a sense of relatedness or belonging, you feel supported in your life. You have social connections that bolster your self-worth and self-confidence. This can improve your emotive state and provide a sense of connectedness through meaningful relationships. Your social connectivity can foster your motivation and goal-related behaviours, making it easier to lead your way towards goal attainment.

Consider how you can build your sense of relatedness. Who can you identify to build relationships with within your workplace? How might you establish connectivity with your colleagues?

Relatedness is often built from pursuing common goals, so finding opportunities to collaborate with others is a good place to start. Where you work in teams, invest some time in understanding who your teammates are. Move from working side by side or above your teammates to working *with* your teammates. By sharing ideas, issues, learnings and questions, you are building trust and creating a collaborative relationship, increasing your sense of belonging. Getting to know other people means they are more likely to get to know you, and once this occurs your professional relationships are likely to blossom.

Relatedness also stems from feeling as though the environment you are working in is one that you belong to. It's about having some familiarity with your workplace. Take some time to learn about your company's values and mission and consider how your values align. Discover the different facets of the organisation to assess how you can eke out your 'home' within it. You may find that, in addition to your work group, there are teams within the organisation with whom you have common interests, such as those focused on social impact, social or sporting clubs, global interest groups, or other technical or industry teams.

Internal social media platforms can also assist you with learning about others within the organisation. Team sites may offer opportunities for you to contribute to discussions or identify other people in the organisation with whom you can build collaborative relationships. Don't underestimate the power of digital communications. You can build your eminence and relationships quickly by engaging with others in such feeds.

Your sense of belonging is likely to grow where you feel included and valued. This of course can depend on how others within the organisation behave. However, you can focus on what you can control, which includes how you bring yourself to engage with others, how proactive you are in building professional relationships and how you seek support from others.

Relationships also take some effort, so give yourself some time to allow them to develop. Dropping past a colleague's office to say hello, share a coffee or meet for lunch can build those connections over time. Don't overlook the opportunities that result from conversations around the water cooler, while making a coffee in the shared kitchen or while standing in line at the printer. Challenge yourself to get to know other colleagues so you have a connection with them and feel a part of the organisation. Volunteering to participate in company-wide projects can create further opportunities to meet others and increase your relatedness.

As your social connections within the work environment increase, you are more likely to grow in confidence, which will support you in pursuing your leadership-related goals.

Self-coaching exercise

Think of a goal you wish to attain. In shaping your goal, reflect on your sense of relatedness and answer the following questions:

- Who can support you with your goal?
- Who might you collaborate with and learn from?
- Who can you turn to for assistance when you don't have all the answers or are lacking confidence in relation to your goal?
- Who might be a part of your cheer squad? Who will encourage you with your goal and celebrate your success?
- Who might challenge you (in a safe way) to help you see what you might not otherwise see?
- What actions can you take to build your relationships with the people you have listed?

Now that you know self-determination theory, how can you apply it in practice? It's all about reflection. You are better off stopping now to assess whether your goals are self-determinant rather than realising far down the track that your progress is slow and laboured. If you want to make progress towards your destination and lead yourself with ease, start with the following exercise.

Self-coaching exercise

Using the goal hierarchy you constructed in Practice 2, ensure that your SMART goals are also self-concordant, values-based goals. Alter the language of each goal from something you *must* do to something you *should* do or would even *like* to do. Rewrite each goal in this form so you are more connected with it and it is more meaningful to you.

Assess your goals to identify how you can be self-determinant. Utilise the questions in the self-coaching exercises within this chapter to ensure your goals are increasing your autonomy, competency and relatedness.

Self-coaching summary

♦ Goals that are aligned with your values are more likely to motivate you.

♦ Goals that align with your personal values are self-concordant goals, which increase your wellbeing.

♦ Reframe your goals from being external (something you *must* do), to introjected (something you *should* do), to identified (something you would *like* to do) and, where possible, to intrinsic (something you would *love* to do).

♦ Self-determination theory supports goal attainment and helps you become more motivated to grow and change.

♦ Ensure your goals are designed to include autonomy, competency and relatedness.

Practice 4

Leading with self-awareness

In a group feedback session I was managing, Jay's name came up again and again. Many a colleague had raised concerns regarding Jay's abrupt manner – yet Jay himself seemed unaware of his impact. There was no doubt that Jay was highly qualified, with numerous degrees and having worked in the industry for some time; yet the harshness of his interactions with others diminished those around him and reduced the team's impact and enjoyment of work. Jay spoke over people and was adamant about his view being the right view. After interacting with Jay, teammates often felt uncomfortable with how they had been spoken to, and some chose to lessen their interactions with him as a result.

'Surely Jay must be aware of how he is coming across!' said a frustrated colleague. Yet Jay wasn't aware. No one had told him about the impact he was having, and he lacked sufficient self-awareness to notice. On the contrary, Jay held himself in high esteem and considered himself to be of great value to the organisation. He enjoyed bringing his skills into play and solving problems that seemed complex to others. He had no realisation that his interactions were disengaging and demoralising others – and with no feedback otherwise, Jay felt at ease continuing on his way.

Too often we lead through our careers without pausing to reflect on how we are actually progressing and the impact we're having. The adage 'I'll just keep doing what I'm doing until someone tells me otherwise' gives others responsibility for your actions. It prevents you from taking the ownership, responsibility and accountability required to make a truly positive impact. This chapter is all about leading with mindful self-awareness.

Why self-reflect?

The best leaders are those who are self-aware. They understand how they impact others, which strengths they can deploy and which traits support or hinder them in their leadership of themselves and others. They use their self-awareness to make better choices and increase their effectiveness in their role.

Self-awareness allows you to be your best self and lead your way effectively. Personal growth and development results when you reflect on your behaviours, emotions and thoughts. Self-awareness requires an intentional shift in gears where you engage in self-reflection and consider your progress, decisions, rationales and choices, and how these impact your leadership and those around you.

By looking in the virtual mirror, you can gain further insights to discover what is working well and where you can improve as you lead your way. Unlike your IQ, emotional intelligence (EQ) can be improved during your lifetime. Researchers have found that developing emotional self-awareness helps us 'improve judgement, develop bonding and connection, and... identify opportunities for professional development and personal growth'.[22]

Self-reflection allows you to identify how you are performing day-to-day under normal working conditions, and also how you perform while under pressure. It can help you discover how you might be limiting your effectiveness through adopting automatic negative thinking, including the imposter syndrome. Perhaps you might discover how effective you are as you interact with others. You can consider how you are utilising strengths, how you are motivating and engaging yourself and others towards your goals, and how you are performing as you lead your way. Through self-reflection you can see how you are setting yourself up for success, or how you are impeding your leadership. It requires more than a passing glance. You must make time for self-discovery and insight.

Self-reflection also supports the choices you make as you lead. You need to focus on what's ahead yet *be aware* of the past. Learning from what you have or have not achieved is an effective way to build your self-awareness. It can help you establish where you need to focus to improve your impact. It also aids you in identifying what has worked well for you in the past and, therefore, what you can draw upon to support further success.

Schedule time – make it happen

In my experience with my coachees, quality self-reflection rarely occurs without them intentionally stopping to do so. Those who prioritise understanding themselves find it easier to lead their way and be their best selves.

Scheduling time each week to reflect on your progress towards your goals provides you with an opportunity to assess yourself. It allows you to adopt an inquiring mind where you can explore your performance, as well as your alignment with your values and purpose. By imposing this time within your weekly routine, you can intentionally draw your attention to yourself and assess your internal self-awareness.[23]

It's as easy as blocking time in your diary. I recommend finding 30 to 60 minutes each week to use as personal reflection time. This investment is less than 1 per cent of your waking hours each week! Make it non-negotiable time so you protect that time slot and build a habit of weekly reflection. For those with electronic diaries, colour-code the allotted time so it doesn't sneak up on you but is something you can see yourself moving towards each week.

Self-coaching exercise

Add a recurring weekly calendar invitation for yourself in your diary called 'Reflection'. Colour-code it so you can easily notice it as you move towards it each week.

Make a firm commitment to utilise these 30 to 60 minutes for your own self-reflection, reviewing how your week has gone.

What does self-reflection entail?

Many people tell me they don't know how to self-reflect. For some it sounds very much like meditation or higher-level thinking. Others consider self-reflection a process yet are stumped by how to go about it.

Self-reflection involves more than simply looking back at yourself. It's more than simple introspection, where you focus on the historical reasons for why you are acting in a particular way or experiencing an emotion. It requires curiosity and inquiry to assess personal progress and understand what is occurring so you can gain insights.

The process I guide my clients through has three steps (as shown in Figure 5). This process can provide you with greater wisdom regarding your own effectiveness.

Figure 5: The self-reflection process

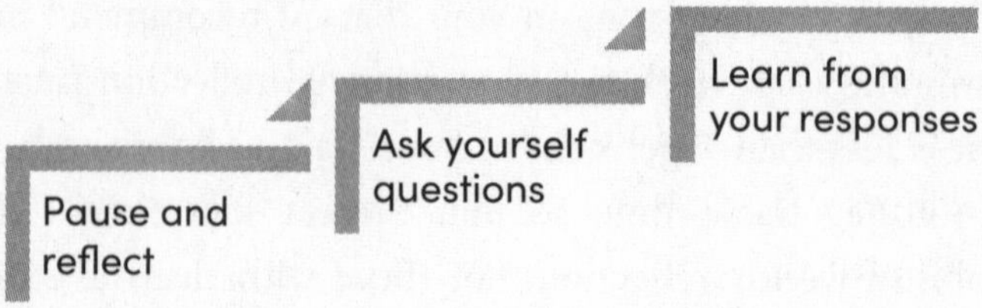

Pause and reflect

Ask yourself questions

Learn from your responses

Self-coaching exercise

Reflect on the questions below and assess your responses to learn more about yourself:

1. What's working well? What am I doing or thinking that is supporting me and allowing for my success? What am I doing or thinking that is supporting my team and allowing for their success?

2. What should I be doing differently? How are my behaviours, emotions and thoughts impeding my success and that of my team?

3. What has triggered my behaviours, emotions and thoughts?

4. What patterns can I see in these behaviours, emotions and thoughts?

5. What choices can I make to select alternative behaviours, emotions and thoughts when these conditions arise to allow for a different (preferable) outcome?

6. How can I utilise my prior success to support my current goals?

7. How am I using my strengths in approaching my goals?

In asking yourself these questions, pay attention to the patterns you can see. Upon reflection, did you notice you have particular emotional responses to certain situations? Were your emotions in proportion to the issue at hand, or did you have an elevated emotional state? Was your 'go-to' state one of defensiveness and excuse-making, or have you approached your goals with an openness of mind, a growth mindset, that allows you to learn and develop?

Be mindful of your unconscious bias where you hesitate to question your state of mind and the basis of your assumptions. Noticing your perspectives will help you to become more adaptive and flexible, reducing related anxiety.[24]

Assumptions, biases and cognitive distortions

We all hold assumptions, biases and beliefs that govern the way we see the world. Becoming self-aware and noticing the stories you tell yourself will help you realise the impact these stories have on your behaviours, emotions and thoughts. The stories may inhibit your behaviours or cause you to act without considering the consequences.

In my coaching experience I've witnessed several cognitive distortions – faulty ways of thinking or negative mindsets – that leaders tend to inhabit. If you are not aware of the assumptions and beliefs you're carrying, you're not able to challenge them – and you can find yourself inhibiting your own performance as a leader. Once you become aware of their existence, you become better able to lead yourself through such thinking, developing restructured thoughts in support of yourself.

Let's take a look at some of the most common cognitive distortions I see in my coaching.

The imposter syndrome

Many high-performing leaders I coach raise concerns about their ability to perform in their role. Although they have been highly successful, they are well regarded as the right person to hold their role and they have delivered value, they are persistently concerned about being found out by a significant other as a fraud or imposter. They fear they have only achieved all they have due to luck, being in the right place at the right time, good fortune, having a strong advocate and so on – not because they are the right person for the job or are sufficiently skilled. They operate in fear that they are about to be found out, will disappoint others, or won't perform or live up to the expectations of the role.

Self-limiting thinking

You may notice your thinking is not supporting you in your role or helping you advance; rather, it is suggesting to you that you are not suited for the role, that you can't do it or won't do it well. You tell yourself that you *should* have known something you missed, or that you're not good enough. You harshly judge yourself and listen to the inner critic who says you should have done it better. You can be your own worst enemy as you underplay your strengths, highlight your weaknesses, replay your mistakes and erode your confidence in support of your belief that you can't do something well.

Catastrophising

You may be thinking the worst, blowing something out of proportion or creating a scenario in your head that is much more serious or concerning than the reality. These catastrophic thoughts might be telling you that you will fail, be demoted or lose your job; that you won't be able to pay your mortgage, will need to sell your house, will be in financial and familial distress, and more. The situation you create is likely to be magnified well beyond what is likely to occur, causing you to pull away from a challenge or opportunity – and feel much distress.

Jumping to conclusions

How often to you find yourself forming a belief with little or no evidence to support it? This commonly arises when you observe or hear of a situation, make assumptions about what you have seen or heard and come to your own conclusions, which creates your beliefs. You infer an outcome based on what you have deduced. How often do you realise that your beliefs are not true once you test your assumptions? Jumping to conclusions may result when you negatively mindread others' thoughts and assume the worst, or crystal-ball-gaze and predict a negative outcome.

Reframing automatic negative thoughts

What is in common in all these cognitive distortions is the nature of what they are: they are *automatic negative thoughts*, and they create self-limiting beliefs. If you are not self-aware, you will believe the stories you tell yourself are true. These stories are neither enabling nor empowering; rather, they limit you to restrictive beliefs. You may find yourself using these stories as excuses for your behaviour, emotions or thoughts, or blaming them for your lack of success.

But let's remember what these are. They are simply stories. Our brains love stories, and they are wired to lean into the negative. We love a drama-filled tale that presents us with the basis of why we are what we are. The more we tell ourselves these negative stories, the more we limit ourselves to what they say is true.

I saw this play out with my coachee Irina. She wanted to have great success in her role but didn't feel she was having the impact she desired. She had only recently been promoted into her senior leadership role. She had more than 20 years of detailed technical experience but found she was rarely speaking up in meetings. The story she told herself was that she was junior to the other leaders in the room and should wait her turn. She thought she needed to earn her stripes before she could interject and share her point of view. She wasn't yet worthy of taking their time or having the floor.

Irina assumed that her behaviour was appropriate and that hierarchy should be respected. As a result, she was limiting her participation and was seen as reserved and unassertive. She was often overlooked for opportunities and felt frustrated, diminished and ineffective as a leader. Irina had started to label herself as such, which was making her feel even more anxious. The more she felt this way, the less she participated. It was becoming a never-ending cycle.

We explored this in detail as I questioned whether Irina's beliefs were true. Was it always true that she should wait her turn? After some hesitation she suggested it was not. There were times when she should speak up and her thoughts would be welcomed. No one had advised her otherwise, and she had set this rule for herself. She was directly impeding her own success because of the stories she had told herself. Her self-limiting thoughts lessened her impact.

We practised an approach to help her move her automatic negative thoughts to realistic thoughts, which I would like to share with you as a self-coaching strategy. This technique is based on a cognitive behavioural model suggesting that what you think influences how you feel, which influences how you behave.[25]

Self-coaching exercise

Utilise this strategy to support yourself in reframing the narrative you tell yourself.

First, build your self-awareness by answering these questions:

1. Notice the story you are telling yourself. What do you hear? (For example, *I am not the right person for this job. My strategic thinking is just not good enough.*)

2. What does it make you think? (*I think that I'm going to fail. I'll be so humiliated.*)

3. How does it make you feel? (*I feel nervous and anxious.*)

4. How does it make you behave? (*I start pulling out of the opportunity and declining invitations to the team meetings.*)

5. How does it help or hinder you in moving towards your goal or being effective as a leader? (*I'm not in attendance, so I'm unable to hear different perspectives about this issue, so my knowledge and insights are limited. My strategic thinking is not improving.*)

Next, reimagine the situation and replace your automatic negative thoughts with realistic positive thoughts. Retell your true story via the following questions:

1. What would be an alternative realistic positive thought that would better support you in this moment? (For example, *I may not yet have all the answers, but I can draw on what I know to date and learn from others. I can develop my strategic thinking.*)

2. What does it make you think? (*I will be challenged but that's okay. I will learn more as I continue with this.*)

3. How does it make you feel? (*I feel open to learning more and recognising my shortcomings. I feel open to learning from others.*)

4. How does it make you behave? *(I am more curious and ask more questions. I consult with others to broaden my perspective.)*

5. How does this help you in moving towards your goal or being effective as a leader? *(I open my boundaries to build my perspective and become more strategic in my decision-making. I test and validate my thinking with my team members and peers and my confidence grows.)*

Commit to action and practise this approach whenever you recognise the automatic negative thoughts arising.

The key to altering your narrative is to become aware of your automatic negative thoughts (your current state) so you can alter your story (your mindset) to move towards your desired state (your truth). What assumptions are you holding, and have you tested their validity? Which part of you is showing up at different times – your inner critic, your need to fit in, your perfectionist tendencies, your fear of people's opinions (FOPO)?

Regular self-reflection will help you notice when you are framing your situation negatively, allowing for your active choices in reframing your position. The sooner you notice your unhelpful thinking, the sooner you can make choices to adopt more helpful thought pathways.

In my coaching experience the most self-aware leaders are those who routinely self-reflect from week to week. They use their regular reflection time to assess the interactions they have had with others and with themselves.

It's only once you have generated your self-awareness that you can take active steps to change behaviours, control emotions and alter your thinking and assumptions. Noticing what you do and intentionally selecting meaningful responses helps you work as your best self. As we critique others' actions we should also be focusing on our own actions to better enable our improved performance. Research has found that 'Accurate self-assessment helps people optimize the capabilities they possess and be aware of those they do not. When you are aware of your strengths and limits, you are more confident about what you can and cannot do. They act as powerful motivators for future performance.'[26]

What do others see?

In addition to noticing what you see in your virtual mirror, asking for feedback to learn how others are seeing you can also improve your self-awareness. Research shows that the way other people see us is more objective than the way we see ourselves.[27] External feedback provides additional perspectives to broaden your own views.

When I was working in my first corporate job, one of my leaders held some views I didn't agree with. His approach to business was unsettling. It wasn't that he was an unsuccessful businessman. In fact, he was very good at what he did. It was just that, with my very few years of experience behind me, I had a level of (perhaps unfair) scepticism about his thought processes and problem-solving skills. Yet I hadn't raised this with him. I thought it was something only I realised.

Then one day, as he was talking to me, he stopped suddenly and with frustration said, 'What is it?! What?' I went into defensive mode, responding, 'What are you talking about?' 'That face!' he said. 'Every time I talk to you, you make that face!'

I knew exactly what he was talking about. My face told a story: a story of scepticism and mistrust. My expressive face displayed a questioning frown and pursed lips, and I hadn't imagined that he had noticed. I was sure that I had internalised my scepticism. Yet his feedback to me was a huge learning. He was able to bring to my attention how he was seeing me. His external feedback broadened my view.

I realised I had a choice to make. I had to either raise my (unfounded) scepticism with him or control my facial expressions to avoid damaging our relationship. I learnt in time to do both! I worked on using my voice to challenge his thinking, and worked on increasing my consciousness around the expressions I was making that obviously made him uncomfortable. I didn't always get it right, but in time I became more at ease and informed. I was able to better trust in him, trust in myself to ask questions so I could understand and evaluate his thinking, and relax my expressions so as to avoid making him feel uncomfortable.

My example here did not arise because I directly asked for feedback; yet the feedback I received did provide me with additional personal insights. A better position is having the courage to *ask* for feedback. Feedback helps you identify blind spots that may be impeding your success.[28] Blind spots are tricky to navigate in leadership, just as they are when you drive your car. They aren't easy to see and can cause some damage if you don't notice them. Having a trusted colleague help you identify your blind spots is invaluable and can provide you with an additional perspective for reflection.

Blind spots can take some time to unpack. Think about how you notice them while driving. It takes mindful attention to focus on a space you otherwise wouldn't readily see. New driving students are taught to do a blind-spot check, where they turn their heads to identify what is otherwise hidden outside of their usual view. Their learning causes them to gather new insights and data and avoid car crashes and disasters. They become mindful of who else is around them and how they might impact that driver, pedestrian or other road user if they don't engage consciously in their driving experience.

My coachee Drayden was assessing their manner of delivering feedback. They thought they were providing feedback effectively, yet had not tested this with anyone. They were frustrated with their team members' reluctance to change and assumed they were being recalcitrant. Drayden told me they used the 'sandwich' approach for feedback – a positive message followed by the negative feedback, followed by another positive message. The negative feedback was sandwiched in between two positive messages. And guess what was occurring? Their team members were only hearing and remembering the positive messages. The negative messages in between were being muted. Drayden's people weren't being difficult; they simply weren't hearing Drayden's feedback due to the way in which it was delivered.

After some coaching (and feedback), Drayden was able to recognise that they held a high level of empathy. They always wanted people to feel good about themselves. This high empathy was challenging Drayden's delivery of direct feedback: they tended to 'sugar-coat' the feedback so as to avoid hurting anyone's feelings. It was only once they became aware of this blind spot that they could start to be mindful of their empathy and build their own skills in delivering feedback. Understanding this blind spot allowed Drayden to communicate very differently with their team members, which supported them in building their skills.

What if you don't like what others see in you? Feedback can lead to feelings of anguish and uncertainty. Yet third-party reflections remain valuable as they provide you with an opportunity to learn from others' insights and follow a pathway that generates new options or actions to better the situation.

It's important to select people who will support you in the feedback process. Dr Tasha Eurich suggests being picky about *who* you ask for feedback: 'You should be confident they want you to be successful; they should have regular exposure to the behaviors you want to learn more about; and they should have a pattern of telling the truth, even when it's difficult for people to hear.'[29]

Self-coaching exercise

Select three people you can ask for feedback regarding your performance and impact. In your notebook, write down their names and the specific area of your performance or impact you would like them to provide feedback on.

Don't wait for feedback. Recognise that people may not have your needs front of mind and may not be proactive in providing you feedback. No doubt they will have some feedback for you when asked, so your role is to seek it. Note too that some people are better at giving feedback than others. You can help them provide you with constructive feedback by providing them with a simple frame: 'What's working well in relation to what I do? What would make it even better?'

How do you receive feedback?

When others give you feedback, take the time to write down and clarify the key points they've raised. Your emotions can blur your recollections of challenging conversations, stifling your ability to clearly recall key messages. Defensiveness, excuse-making or a closed mindset can be roadblocks that hinder your ability to receive feedback. Don't waste the gift of the feedback. Be present when it is delivered, unpack it and cherish the lessons that come with it to better yourself.

I like to visualise feedback as a gift – perhaps in a blue Tiffany & Co box wrapped with a big ribbon. There are many dimensions to gift giving. There is typically a level of thoughtfulness associated with gift giving; usually, the giver has taken some time to consider what might be the best thing to place in the gift box. It's the same with the gift of feedback. The person giving the feedback is presenting you with something that is hopefully thoughtful and has some value.

Open the gift with curiosity and inquiry. Unpack it to discover more. When you open a gift box and discover it's full of wrapping paper, you would be unlikely to stop there. You'd go further to discover what's inside. It's the same with your receipt of feedback. Unpack the feedback to uncover more. What does it entail? What's underneath the wrapping paper? What does the feedback actually look and sound like?

Be mindful of the gesture of gift giving. Typically, people present a gift with positive intention. Try to receive the gift of feedback with gratitude rather than suspicion or defensiveness, even if the feedback is initially surprising or unexpected. Try to learn from the gift you have been given.

Adopting an open mind with a growth mindset best positions you to assess feedback. If you don't agree with the feedback you've received, consider whether it is actually a blind spot – something you can't see in yourself. Don't quickly dismiss it. Instead, discuss the feedback with others to see if it is something they can also see in you. This can help provide further depth to the significance of the feedback and give you insight into whether it's a potential blind spot.

When you reflect on feedback, create learning goals that provide you with opportunities to effect change and move towards an improved outcome. What are your key learnings or takeaways from the feedback? How can you advance your impact with these learnings? How are the learnings meaningful to you and others?

If the feedback is vague or generalised, ask questions to better understand the meaning. 'Mine' the feedback: dig deeply into it to ensure you have struck gold. If all you are left with is darkness, you need to dig deeper to better understand what the other person is trying to communicate.

My coachees often report to me that they are told they are 'on track' or 'doing well'. Sometimes they are told to 'keep doing what they are doing'. When I ask them what that means, too many coachees say they don't know; that's all the feedback they received. This highlights a deficiency in the feedback delivery. They haven't been given any feedback of consequence, so no learnings come from it. This makes it challenging to build self-awareness.

This type of feedback might feel neutral or even positive, but it isn't particularly helpful. It's hard to learn from it when it is non-specific. I recommend seeking examples related to the feedback to better contextualise it. You could ask for examples of specific behaviours that illustrate the traits the feedback-giver would like to see in you to assist with your understanding of what the behaviours look like in action. Or, ask for examples of situations specific to you that evidence the feedback. The more you inquire and *mine* the feedback, the better off you will be.

Self-coaching exercise

The next time you receive non-specific feedback, ask the following open questions to mine that feedback for context and meaning:

- What's an example of someone who does that really well, so I can learn from their approach?
- What would be an example of when you saw me at my best? What was positive about that?
- What about an example of when you thought I could improve my performance? What should I focus on as a result?
- What should I focus on in our next task to ensure that my performance improves even more?
- What would you say I should do more of, and what should I do less of?
- If you were me, what would you focus on the most to make the greatest impact?
- What feedback do you have from others who have worked with me? Have they shared their experience, and what can I learn from that?
- Who should I connect with to learn more about how to improve in that development area?

The feedback you receive when you mine for meaning may help you increase your self-regulation, enhance your self-control and manage impulses and emotions. You may learn to adapt your behaviours and cognitions in response to differing situations and apply new perspectives and critical thinking to better your outcomes.

Invest in yourself and get to know yourself better. When you learn about yourself and also see what others see in you, you will have greater opportunities to be your best self and lead your way with impact.

Self-coaching summary

- Self-awareness is developed through self-reflection and seeking feedback from others.
- Increased self-awareness improves how you lead your way.
- Schedule weekly time to engage in self-reflection. Ask yourself key questions to consciously consider how you are behaving, feeling and thinking. What were the consequences (intended and unintended) of your actions? What have you learnt from your reflections?
- Notice the stories you are telling yourself and assess whether they are helping or hindering you.
- Mindfully engage in self-analysis to determine which behaviours, emotions and thoughts you might like to alter.
- Seek feedback from trusted others. Take notes and remain present to absorb their insights. Return the favour by giving them feedback.
- Consider your blind spots and assess how best to respond to them.
- If you receive non-specific feedback, use questioning to mine that feedback for the gold.

Practice 5

Managing your time

At the beginning of our Zoom coaching session Terry immediately started talking about how he had just come off a conference call that went way over time. His Executive had decided that a major project deadline must be brought forward by two weeks. Terry needed to address some key issues to make this happen, so he was keen to dive into our coaching call quickly and perhaps clip 15 minutes off the end. This would allow him to draft and send some emails about the project before his next appointment.

Terry spoke in swift sentences with matching hand gestures. His body language suggested heightening anxiety as his brain tried to process all that he was carrying. He was conscious that his day was back-to-back with meetings. His diary looked like a solid block of colour with no white space available for creative thought or spontaneous catch-ups. He knew his team members were queuing at his virtual door to spend time with him, yet he didn't see how he could fit them in this week. He was crossing his fingers that they would work things out for themselves while he managed his physical and mental load. It was hectic!

Although Terry had a PA, Leon, working with him, he hadn't invested any time sharing his priorities with him, which challenged

Leon as further meeting requests came through. Leon did his best to make judgement calls, but Terry was often too busy to connect with him and calibrate the list of meeting requests with what Terry regarded as urgent, important or of little relevance to his goals. Leon did his best to fit what he could in Terry's heaving diary and waited for his feedback.

Terry described himself as busy. 'How are you, Terry?' I managed to ask. 'Busy!' he spat back. 'I'm so busy!'

Terry's busy state created an interesting dilemma. In an ideal world you can lead your way towards your goals, determining when and how you focus on achieving them. As we learnt in Practice 3, using self-determination to approach your goals enables you to be your best self and lead your way.

However, an ideal world is often far from the reality you experience. Like Terry, in reality you will be immersed in a busy work environment, where your professional goals are wedged alongside other colleagues', teams' and leaders' priorities. Their agendas may interfere with your ideal use of time, making it challenging to remain focused on how you most effectively lead your way.

In this practice we'll look at some self-coaching strategies to support you in your busy state. We'll highlight how you prioritise your time and agenda in the midst of the many other priorities that come your way. We'll also consider some strategies you can utilise to best manage how you dedicate your time and lead your way towards your goals.

How being busy impacts your leadership

Within the workplace you will find an ever-growing list of things to do, places to be and people to see. The boundaries of our working days tend to stretch with the accessibility of technology and communication. We are presented with lots of choices within shortened time frames, all of which create different focal points of attention. Our capacity to act is reduced as we jump between choices at increasing pace in a constant state of being busy.

Being busy is a topic often raised in my executive coaching forums. It's a response to why goals have not been achieved. My coachees cite being busy as the reason they have lost their focus. They feel like their wheels are spinning as they attempt to lead themselves towards their goals.

Conversations with friends and colleagues often sound like this: 'Hi, how are you?' 'SO busy! What about you?' 'Yep, me too – busy.' Conversation done. A nod of the head; a look of shared understanding. There's no time to share much more. We're busy!

Being busy has become the new vogue. Some may say if you're not busy you're neither important nor effective. If you ask someone how they are, without a thought they'll often reply 'Busy!' It's a badge of honour.

Studies demonstrate that 'displaying one's busyness at work and lack of leisure time operates as a visible signal of status in the eyes of others'. The positive status effect of displaying busyness is driven by the perception that a busy person 'possesses desired human capital characteristics (competence, ambition)' and is in demand in the job market.[30]

In a competitive landscape, status can be important; but let's slow down and reconsider this. Are you able to be your best self and lead your way when you adopt a busy state? Does being busy and having perceived status really mean that you are a better leader?

Busyness and collaboration

Your career becomes very self-centred when it occurs in a state of constant busyness. Little time remains for collaboration. Collaboration is full of potential opportunities to build and maintain relationships, which is key to leading as your best self.

Being time poor has led to people feeling 'too busy' to share their knowledge when requested, reducing collaboration and opportunities to learn from others.[31] This reflects poorly on you as a leader and is not an optimal state to adopt. A myopic view of the landscape can only lead to limited perspectives. Collaboration opens you to multiple perspectives and creative thinking. It can broaden your insights and allow you to be better informed and lead more effectively at your best. It can help you achieve your goals. It can also strengthen your own perspective and support the direction you are taking, or provide you with options to select an alternative, preferable direction.

It's useful to understand the many benefits of being mindful of your busy state and slowing down to share your knowledge. Doing so will increase your professional profile and support your fame agenda, drawing your expertise to others' attention. In sharing your knowledge you'll extend your network and build relationships that can benefit your career and inform your approach to leadership. The stronger your relationships, the greater your likelihood of finding support when you need it. Collaborative acts positively build your reputation, increasing your chances of being at the forefront of others' minds and being offered opportunities to advance your experience and enjoyment of what you do.

Busyness and creativity

All leaders need time to think. Leadership requires you to move from being in the detail to big-picture thinking. You need to find time to invest in yourself to alter your perspective. If you are too busy to invest this time, you will be less likely to challenge the status quo. You will find yourself repeating errors. You will be less able to differentiate yourself and move towards innovative thinking. When you become too busy, you are less likely to alter your behaviours and thinking to learn and grow.

Activity versus productivity

Jumping from one priority to the next in a hectic, multitasking way might make you feel as though you have your fingerprint on many things and have everything under control. However, your ability to be focused, productive and effective is diminished. Don't confuse activity with productivity. Performance is actually lessened when you are multitasking compared to when you complete tasks sequentially.[32] Increased multitasking also leads to a significant decrease in accuracy, which can negatively impact your performance.[33]

'Is that really true?' you may ask as you read this. Well, stop and ask yourself: what are you currently doing? Yes, I mean now – in this moment. List all the things you have been doing for the last 30 minutes while you read this book. How many tasks did you count?

What did you notice about what you were just doing, and how much of it was conscious or unconscious? Did you even notice yourself pausing your reading while you scrolled through your phone or email, tidied your desk, thought about the report you are completing, ticked off your long task list or sipped your freshly brewed coffee? How did this impact your ability to be present and focused?

Well, why don't you test it? Reflect on how much you have read in this chapter and how much you have actually absorbed. To be fair, you've probably picked up a considerable amount; yet how efficiently have you done so? Being an evidence-based coach I like to draw on research, which in this case suggests that performing several tasks at the same time can reduce productivity by as much as 40 per cent. It can overload the brain. The human brain needs to accumulate information continuously across time. Interruptions that require switching your attention to other event sequences disrupt this process.[34] Your ability to remain focused can be diminished, which makes it more challenging to achieve your goals.

It is also possible that your busy state might cause you to disengage from your work, which will poorly impact your goal attainment. Disengagement is characterised by 'a deferring of the request to another time, a physical withdrawal from work, and a reprioritization of tasks, others and self', all of which can arise when you are too busy to stop and participate or engage in your work.[35] Even small yet important tasks, such as resetting passwords, may be overlooked by busy multitaskers, increasing the risk of career-sensitive information being shared.[36]

Apply the brakes

Now that you understand that being busy does not mean that you are productive, how can you take stock of this and regain your focus?

The first step is to become mindful of what is currently on your plate. Assess your priorities and determine what you can say no to, rather than saying yes to all that comes your way. The easiest way to do this is to focus on what matters to you – your purpose. As we saw in Practice 1, this is the basis of *why* you do what you do. Once you are able to articulate this, you will be able to correlate your priorities against what gives you meaning, energy and engagement in your role.[37] You will find it easier to stay focused on your goals.

Simon Sinek suggests that you 'start with why' to understand why you do what you do, rather than simply focusing on the *what* and *how*. [38] As we saw in Practice 1, articulating your *why* helps you and others differentiate what your purpose is, what you stand for and what gives you meaning. It's often an emotional, values-based connection to why you do what you do. Once identified, your *why* provides an internal navigation system that can help you apply the brakes on your busyness. It can support you in your decision to say no to different demands on your time and help you set your priorities so that you can remain focused on your goals.

Another way to consider your purpose is to identify the meaning it creates for you. Zach Mercurio, who we discussed in Practice 1, talks about focusing on the impact you want to make and why this matters to you.[39] Then, correlate this with how you prioritise your time.

Once your purpose is clear, it becomes much easier to assess different opportunities and focus on the commitments that give you the most meaning and motivation. Identifying and prioritising purposeful activities will ensure that what you are engaging in is energising and motivating and produces positive emotions. This will make it easier for you to lead your way, as you are more likely to feel more optimism and hope, be more creative and engaged, and experience improved wellbeing and performance. This insight can support your choice to say no to activities that do not align with your purpose and that are both time-consuming and less meaningful. You can own your time, rather than having others own it. You can aim to engage the greater amount of your professional time undertaking tasks and activities that have meaning and align with your purpose.

It is of course important to recognise that there will be activities you need to engage in that are not as purposeful but are a necessary requirement of your role. For instance, you may be most engaged and purposeful when you are designing creative business solutions for your clients, and least engaged and purposeful when you are completing the associated administration and billing, yet the administration activities are a necessary component of your role and are necessary to enable the creative work you most enjoy. These less purposeful activities are those you *must do*.

Realistically, you can't operate in a vacuum and only engage in activities that are entirely purposeful. To do so would assume that you have complete choice and ability to elect how you use your time without any influence from others. Most of us work within organisations that require us to participate in various roles, some of which may require us to complete less purposeful tasks than others. Career sustainability requires a level of acceptance of and patience towards these tasks. Yet, rather than mindlessly adding to your list of must-do tasks, you can turn your mind to seeking support with them. It's about engaging in effective delegation (we'll discuss this in more detail in Practice 9). You may find you are delegating to someone who finds purpose and meaning in these activities, and as a result you have bolstered *their* engagement with their career (this is an effective way to lead others). You can pass on, or *offload*, some of your must-do activities and revert to more purposeful activities yourself. It's a win-win scenario.

Once you delegate, you have released yourself from the time and headspace required to undertake that task, allowing yourself more time to engage in more purposeful activities – all because you stopped saying yes to everything and started to think purposefully.

Figure 6 is a useful tool for assessing and prioritising the many tasks and goals you have. You can assess each task and goal against the three frames, noting which are most purposeful, which are must-dos and which you can pass on. The hope is that you can focus most of your time on the most purposeful goals and reduce the amount of time you're spending on the must-do activities by moving them into the pass on frame.

Figure 6: Prioritisation tool

Most purposeful

This is your most productive zone and where you will benefit from focusing.

Devoting a large amount of time to purposeful goals and tasks leads to your highest motivation, engagement, energy, flow and optimism.

These are the goals and tasks you are likely to be most excited about. They matter most to you and provide you with the most fulfilment and meaning.

Must-do

These are the goals and tasks that need to be completed as part of your role but don't align so closely with your purpose. You will have a lower level of motivation and engagement with these goals and tasks. They do absorb your time, however, which may take your focus away from your purposeful goals and tasks.

How can you work through what can't be delegated quickly and efficiently?

What can be done to reframe the goals to align them with your purpose?

Pass on

This is your least productive zone. These are the things you can more readily delegate so you can regain your focus elsewhere.

Identify who else might be motivated to undertake these goals and tasks. They may in fact align with someone else's purpose, so you may be empowering them through delegation. How can you delegate, expand resources or reprioritise to allow you to focus on more purposeful goals and tasks?

Some of my coachees use this tool each week as they review where their focus lies and how they are using their time against their priorities. Completing the chart helps them visualise how their time is being used and supports their choices to free up their time and engage in more purposeful activities. It helps them establish what is keeping them busy and whether this helps or hinders them in leading their way towards the completion of their goals.

Self-coaching exercise

In your notebook, plot your current goals and tasks within each frame of the prioritisation tool. Note down some actions you can take to focus on the tasks in the most purposeful frame while moving tasks from the must-do frame into the pass on frame.

Planful pausing

Leaders who are planful in pausing become more planful. If you plan time in which to pause, you are more likely to use these pauses to plan what you need to do. Starting your day with a pause can help you plan your tasks and decide where you need to focus and devote your time. Don't just jump in and see what the day brings. Bring some planful thinking to your day.

Planning reduces duplication of effort as you can get it right the first time after some mindful decision-making. You become more effective in how you use your time and how you involve others. Planning helps you shape your perspective of what is truly urgent rather than simply important. It also lets you pinpoint tasks and goals to delegate to others in your team. It situates you high above your task list to give you a new perspective on why you are so busy.

Planning cuts through that feeling of being overwhelmed or just too busy. You have time to assess your priorities and put your delegation decisions into action. You can make a plan to sprint through the must-dos and pass on applicable tasks as soon as practicable so that you have more time to spend on your purposeful goals and tasks.

Try a new approach of starting your day with an overview of your prioritisation tool, and then pause for reflection to plan how you will approach your actions to have greater control of your time. Of course, you must allow for some flexibility and agility to respond to unexpected issues that come to your attention; but time is one thing you can't get back, so make the best use of it.

Additionally, you can block time in your diary to make space for differing priorities, including critical thinking, quality assurance and review, marketing and business development, coaching and mentoring, administration and training, social activities, external commitments, wellbeing and lunch breaks, and buffers between meetings. This doesn't mean that your time becomes *locked* in your diary. Rather, you can pause and consider whether you should alter your time commitment in response to clashes. Your planful approach allows you to control what's important to you in how you use your time.

Learning to say no

Maria struggled to say no. She had a deep fear of letting people down and missing opportunities – both FOPO, which we discussed in Practice 4, and fear of missing out (FOMO). These coupled together created an enormous burden and increased Maria's anxiety as she headed towards burnout. It was only once she started to experiment with saying no, and talked about her limited capacity to act, that she started to gain control of her work life and where she focused her time. She improved her ability to focus on the things that mattered to her and was better able to attribute time towards her purposeful goals. Maria's state went from overwhelmed to productive.

I'm not suggesting it happened overnight. It took practice and reflection for her to recognise the impact of her decisions to willingly take on more work without thought, versus pausing to consider whether it made sense for her to do so. Could she fit the task into her already full schedule? What would be the consequences (intended and unintended) for her and her team? Would she diminish her focus on her purposeful goals and priorities if she continued to say yes to every request that was made?

In time Maria built her confidence and ease in saying no and found herself able to develop a more sustainable working rhythm. Her wellbeing improved, as did her enjoyment of her work. She found space to focus on what gave her energy and joy, rather than doing things based on FOPO or FOMO.

Discovering your voice that enables you to say no can be life-changing. For some, the word comes easily. For others there's concern about disappointing others, being left out of future opportunities, not being seen as a team player or having no option but to say yes. Some people are overly concerned about being liked and believe that saying no will cast them in poor light. There's both a sense of obligation and a deference to those who have asked them, and a fear of being poorly viewed.

How do you say no?

Before you jump in and say yes, take a moment to pause. Use that moment to stop your kneejerk reaction of being agreeable, and instead use it to consider the request. Take stock of what you have currently committed to and how this may impact you. What are the consequences of saying yes? Are you comfortable with these, or would your wellbeing improve by declining the request?

If you are unable to simply say 'No thanks, I'm unable to help you with that', choose alternative language. Explaining that you simply don't have capacity to act at this point in time can be a helpful alternative to saying no while supporting your pushback of their request. Explaining that you don't have the time to do justice to the project or task helps to express your concern for a quality outcome.

I also suggest acknowledging the importance of their request and the gratitude you have for them involving you. For instance, you could respond with something like:

Thanks for thinking to involve me. It does sound like a great opportunity. Unfortunately, I am overcommitted with other projects and don't have capacity to take this on. I don't want to over-promise and let you down by agreeing to be involved, so I will have to say no.

Suggesting alternative colleagues for the opportunity can also help the other person to consider accessing further support.

What are your boundaries?

Considering your boundaries is another way to assess whether the request fits within your wheelhouse. If you are being asked to do something that is better suited to another colleague, volunteer this information, and share that the task is not suited to your expertise.

Don't simply take something on because you have been asked. It is possible that the person making the request misunderstands your role or expertise and would benefit from having you bring this to their attention. A useful way to discover this is to dial up your curiosity and ask questions to explore the context of what is being asked of you and from you. You may soon learn that your colleague has not understood your expertise or your areas of focus, which will support you redirecting them to others.

If they still encourage you to carry it, ask yourself whether this is the right thing to do. Would it be the best solution, or simply a convenient one for your colleague as they have solved their problem and delegated to you? If it's the latter, be wise to this and stand your ground.

Also consider your boundaries in terms of time management. Even if you *are* the right person for the project, be curious and question the expected time commitment. The size and complexity of a project described as 'small' or 'short' is relative to the person's expectations of those descriptions. Engage in further inquiry to move to a common understanding of the time frames before agreeing to be involved.

How are you valuing your time for all aspects of your life, including work? How are you fitting in time for family, friends, hobbies, sport, travel and of course (and most importantly) time just for you?

What boundaries do you need to create regarding how you give away your time to others? These can assist you with saying no. My coachee Maria learnt to share her important and purposeful priorities with her team so that they understood the basis of her saying no to requests that required her time before 9 am. She needed this time to drop her son at daycare and travel to the office. Agreeing to early morning meetings that clashed with this caused her stress and challenge in making additional arrangements for her son. It was a horrible way to start her day and caused anxiety for her son, too.

Once she started to communicate this priority to her team members, she felt at ease saying no to these early morning requests, as everyone understood the basis of her decision. In fact, Maria was able to role model this with other team members, who also started to openly discuss their competing priorities and their need to guard particular time slots across their working day. Engagement grew as people felt more empowered and trusted. They also felt more respected as flexibility was relied upon to adjust to competing priorities where possible.

Make space and empty your cup

Another strategy is to consider what you will have to give up to make space for an opportunity you have been offered. Visualise a cup being filled. If you add more to your cup, eventually there will be no space left and you will need to offload something to make room for new tasks.

Offloading may mean finishing some projects before you add more to your cup. It could also mean pouring some out of your cup by sharing responsibilities with other team members, or perhaps pausing existing commitments and setting them aside until you can make room for them in your cup again.

Leading your way means enjoying your professional journey. Try not to forget that. If you are always doing things in response to other people's agendas rather than your own values and priorities, the journey may be bumpy and unsustainable. Most leadership journeys have some level of compromise and complexity, so I'm not asking you to tolerate only perfection. I'm suggesting you be mindful of creating a work life that is meaningful, enjoyable and sustainable, and gives you time to enjoy the ride. Don't get so swamped in your workload that you lose sight of the goals that mean the most to you.

Self-coaching summary

♦ Being busy does not mean being productive.
♦ Busyness can lead to a self-centred state where you have no time to collaborate with others.
♦ Being too busy to stop can reduce your creativity and potential to grow.
♦ Slow down and reflect.
♦ Identify your purpose and how you spend your time against your most purposeful goals and tasks, those you must do and those you can offload.
♦ Lightly planning your day means better use of time.
♦ Time blocking within your diary supports your preferred use of your time.
♦ Effective delegation requires your mindful attention, but it gives you back time to invest in what matters most.
♦ Reflect on how comfortably you say no to requests from others. Note how it impacts your ability to remain focused on fulfilling your goals.

Practice 6

Managing your energy

Many corporate leaders I coach reveal how depleted they feel. They are working long and hard each week, with little time for themselves. Their virtual battery packs tend to run them through to the weekend, when they then plug themselves back in to recharge for the following week.

Too often I have coaching conversations with leaders who are run-down and fatigued and unsure how they can sustain this way of life. There is no question that this presents a significant life challenge for many. How can you expect to live a fulfilled and engaged life when you are maintaining a baseline of depletion and exhaustion? How can you possibly lead your way as your best self in this state?

The best leaders focus on managing their energy stores to avoid depletion. Ada was one such leader. She recognised that she needed to look after her energy so she could lead as her best self. For her to perform in her role, she needed to be in tune with her physical and mental wellbeing and make regular adjustments to rebalance as required. Rather than letting herself move towards a physically or mentally depleted state, Ada built rituals into her day and week to support her wellbeing. These rituals helped maintain her energy state to enable sustained performance.

Ada adopted this approach following one of our coaching sessions when I introduced her to a fabulous study by Jim Loehr and Tony Schwartz. The *Harvard Business Review* article I shared with her compared a sporting athlete preparing themselves for peak performance with a leader working in a corporation.[40] In the article, Loehr and Schwartz describe what can be achieved when we increase our own self-awareness and approach to our working life by focusing on four components, as shown in Figure 7.

Figure 7: Four components of energy management

ADAPTED FROM J LOEHR AND T SCHWARTZ, 'THE MAKING OF A CORPORATE ATHLETE', *HARVARD BUSINESS REVIEW*, 2001, 79(1):120–129, <HBR.ORG/2001/01/THE-MAKING-OF-A-CORPORATE-ATHLETE>.

Loehr and Schwartz's model suggests that to achieve an ideal performance state we need to move regularly between different levels of energy to avoid energy depletion and burnout. We must move from energy expenditure to energy renewal, from stress to recovery. Learning to regularly oscillate between different states of energy enhances performance.

Physical, emotional, mental and spiritual capacity can all be recovered by incorporating rituals and habits that are intentionally scheduled and practised. Rather than waiting until the end of the working week to re-energise, you can adopt rituals during each day that support you in reaching your ideal performance state. You can plan to recover your energy across the day to keep you sustained and firing, allowing you to maintain your physical and mental wellbeing and better lead your way.

Rituals should be developed against all four components: physical, emotional, mental and spiritual capacity. Adopting these rituals as part of your self-coaching strategy will support you in managing your energy and leading as your best self. Let's take a look at each component in detail.

Physical capacity

Your endurance and recovery relies on your body as your energy source. Maintaining your physical capacity promotes physical and emotional recovery, aiding energy renewal and improving your performance.[41]

Designing daily rituals for the following three key constituent parts (and self-coaching against them) will build your physical capacity and wellbeing.

Nutrition

Regular nutritious meals and healthy snacks will fuel your energy source. Prepare some healthy snacks that you can readily access during the day, such as fruits and vegetables, a handful of almonds, a yoghurt, and dips such as hummus or avocado and crackers.[42] As nice as sugary treats can be, they tend to quickly inflate and then drop your insulin levels, causing fatigue. Biscuits, sweets and chocolates might feel like a short-term fix for fatigue, but overindulgence may create other health issues such as weight gain, blood pressure issues and diabetes over time.

My coachee Ada recognised that she was skipping meals and living on coffee. Too many leaders overlook their nutritional requirements in this way. Just as your car requires petrol and oil to function (or maybe electricity if you've managed to buy an electric vehicle!), your body requires healthy food to perform at its best.

Sleep

Many studies have demonstrated the positive impact of regular patterns of at least eight hours of sleep per night. Be aware of your sleep bank and notice if you have made too many withdrawals.

Studies show that 42 per cent of leaders only have six or fewer hours of sleep per night.[43] This means many leaders are operating in a less-than-productive state, with the ripple effect impacting their teams and others around them.[44] Being fatigued can result in mood swings, reduced memory and absorbing information at a slower pace. This is not a preferred state to lead your way. Getting enough sleep is the most obvious way to tackle fatigue and build up your energy.

Build some rituals to prepare yourself for sleep, such as disconnecting from technology at least an hour before you intend to sleep (and leaving your phone outside your bedroom), monitoring the temperature of your room (16 to 18 degrees Celsius is said to be a preferable sleeping temperature), creating a darkened room to relax the body through the release of melatonin and selecting a time to sleep that allows you to sleep for around eight hours per night.

Building your sleep routine will renew your energy and better support your capacity for schematic thinking, memory functioning and interpersonal responses, which will increase your overall performance.[45]

Exercise

Engaging in regular exercise is shown to increase physical and mental energy. The definition of 'regular' differs for us all, but it is suggested that 30-minute sessions of moderate-intensity cardiovascular exercise five days per week coupled with two sessions of strength training each week can support a healthy lifestyle – and, of course, renew your energy levels.[46]

Exercising in 'green space' has additional health benefits, including an increase in wellbeing, changes to your attentional focus helping to reduce stress, and savouring of the environment, which increases your positive emotions.

Fatigue may be reduced by taking short breaks throughout your working day. Moving yourself away from your desk allows for energy replenishment and a change in focus. This can reinvigorate your capacity to focus on your return to work and reduce feelings of fatigue.

Ada took regular ten-minute breaks in which she walked around the office, her home or outside, or did some stretches. We referred to these as 'exercise snacks'! You might find other reasons to get away from your desk, such as refilling your water bottle to stay hydrated. It's about building in a ritual of changing your physical state and altering your attentional focus, which supports your wellbeing.

Emotional capacity

You are a human as well as a leader. It sounds obvious, doesn't it? Yet too many leaders forget that as human beings they will experience the ups and downs of emotions throughout their lives, let alone their weeks. Different environmental issues might trigger certain emotions. Understanding how to support your emotional state can sustain your leadership.

Your emotions create an internal climate that drives your performance state. Feelings of optimism, engagement, calm, excitement, hope, confidence and courage can increase your positive energy stores. Additional positive experiences can broaden your creativity, curiosity, playfulness and ability to create innovative solutions to challenging problems.

On the other hand, feelings of worry, stress, anxiousness, depression, frustration, anger and disillusion can deplete energy stores. This can narrow your focus of attention, making it more difficult to resolve issues.

Ada and I worked through several rituals to assist her with building her emotional capacity. Let's take a look at them.

Noticing, naming and acting on emotions

This self-coaching strategy requires mindful attention to your emotional state. *Notice* what is triggering your emotional response. *Name* the emotion. *Accept* that the emotion is present and *choose* to respond in a way that supports your desired emotional state. Don't let your emotions take you to an outcome you don't desire.[47]

It is often suggested that we need to deal with negative emotions and move on from them quickly; but sometimes our emotions are actually energising and supporting us. The Dalai Lama frames this well:

> *Feeling angry can, in the short term, make our minds more focused and give us an extra burst of energy and determination. However, when anger extends beyond this practical function most of the energy it brings us is not helpful.*[48]

Reflect on what tends to trigger your emotional state and practise this approach for self-support. Your mindful attention to your emotions and the choices you make in response can make a difference to your energy state.

For example, Ada noticed that she was often triggered by a certain colleague's continued questioning of her. She was able to name her emotion, stating it as frustration. She accepted that this was coming up for her in these moments. She chose to be curious and ask her colleague why her actions were concerning him. She used the negative emotion of frustration to focus her attention, and then chose to alter her mental state to one of curiosity. As Ada explained, moving from frustrated to curious helped her shift her mindset and emotional state, which supported her to respond in a more energy-affirming way.

A further self-coaching strategy is to question whether your current emotions and energy levels match your intended activity.

For example, if you are feeling zestful and enthusiastic with high energy, consider whether this matches your intention to engage in deep, focused thought. Is now the best time to author a considered piece of thought leadership, or would you be better off engaging in a high-energy activity, such as networking, which would allow you to channel your energy accordingly?

Pausing to check in on your emotional energy levels will allow you to make informed choices around your leadership activities.

Consider the stories you are telling yourself

We spoke about the stories we tell ourselves in Practice 4. These stories also impact our energy, so it's important to actively select the stories you choose to listen to. Is it positive self-talk or negative self-talk?

Ada discovered that she often told herself she wasn't good enough and wasn't the right person for the job. Together we practised positive self-talk, where she reframed her mental position whenever those thoughts arose. Ada altered her story and repeated to herself: 'You are well qualified for this job and learning every day. You add value to your team and clients.' She found this came easily to her after some practice, and the ritual helped her balance her emotions. Speaking to herself in the second person also supported her confidence and feelings of hope and optimism, as she spoke to herself as a coach or mentor would. She was able to stand outside of herself and offer support and wisdom.

Take note of the language you use and think about how you are feeding your story with negative language. I like to reference this old parable as a useful way to conceptualise this:

A grandfather is telling his grandson a story.

'Grandson, there are two wolves which fight within us, and these same wolves fight within all of us.

'The first wolf is mean, frustrated, angry, sad and hostile. He is sceptical, demeaning and pessimistic.

'The second wolf is kind, calm and considered. He is optimistic, caring and compassionate.'

'Which wolf wins?' the grandson asks.

'The one you feed', he answers.[49]

Give your dog a cuddle

Studies have shown that pet ownership can lead to better psychological wellbeing, lower rates of depression and stress, and increased self-esteem.[50]

Who would have thought that your furry friend could bring you so much?

My cavoodle, Charlie, has been a huge support to me in balancing my emotional state. His capacity for unconditional love is extraordinary!

Express gratitude

Seek out the positive things you are grateful for to reduce your negative emotions. Research supports an increase in your positive emotional state when you're grateful, with resulting self-improvement.[51]

When things don't go as well as you'd hoped, reflect on what is good in your life to regain your perspective. List the top three things you are grateful for at the end of each day. It might be as simple as having had a tasty barista coffee, avoiding a traffic jam on the way to work or finishing a project that had been weighing you down.

My coachee Ada told me she enjoyed doing this with her family each night. Even when her kids gave the same answers, with their top three things being recess, lunchtime and coming home from school, she would giggle with them and then share hers, often weaving in how they had been a part of what she was grateful for. She found it positively impacted her family dynamic as well as her own emotional state.

Positive emotions are furthered when you communicate gratitude to another person and show them why they matter. Ada made a monthly note in her diary to remind herself to share thanks with her team and colleagues. This prompt allowed her to stop and consider who was worthy of gratitude for their contribution to the team, clients and others. She enjoyed reaching out to them and expressing her gratitude with examples of their impact. Who can you choose to express gratitude to today?

Show compassion for yourself and others

Self-compassion researcher Kristin Neff says: 'Self-compassion is an emotionally positive self-attitude that should protect against the negative consequences of self-judgement, isolation, and rumination (such as depression)'.[52]

Talk to yourself as you would a close friend and express kindness and compassion for your current situation. Be forgiving of yourself and understanding of your circumstances.

Ada told me how she found self-compassion useful in resetting her perspective. When she spoke to herself in a compassionate way she became more understanding of herself and the challenges she faced, and stopped being so hard on herself. This allowed her to rethink what and who could support her in the moment. It also allowed her to build resilience, positive emotions and hope.

When I was working with Ada I shared a technique that I had heard Sheryl Sandberg and positive psychologist Adam Grant both use. I asked Ada to think of three things she had done well each day. This is different to identifying things you are grateful for, because it focuses on what you are achieving rather than what others are doing or what isn't working. It helps you recognise what you are capable of.

One example Ada shared with me was beautiful in its simplicity:

- She had a positive conversation with a colleague.
- She said no to participating in an initiative unrelated to her most purposeful goals.
- She reminded herself that she was on her way to success and used positive self-talk.

Now it's your turn to use self-compassion.

Self-coaching exercise

Identify three things that you are grateful for today. Write them in your notebook and savour how these make you feel.

Suggest to your colleagues, team members and family members that they do the same to aid them in managing their emotions.

Now write down three things you have done well today. Which of your strengths have supported you? What have you learnt about yourself from your success?

Music interventions

Short-term music interventions of 10 to 15 minutes can impact your mental and physical wellbeing. Listening to music can provide a distraction from stress-increasing thoughts or feelings, and can reduce obsessive thinking and worrying.[53]

Music has also been found to impact the cardiovascular system, including lowering heart rate and blood pressure. It also lowers cortisol levels, reducing stress.[54]

Being in this altered state can boost your energy levels.

I'm a fan of music from the 1970s and 1980s. A bit of disco gets the blood pumping! Grab your phone and create a playlist to enjoy.

Self-coaching exercise

Arm yourself with the tools you need. Download some music to your phone or subscribe to a streaming service so you have music available when you need a positive emotional boost.

Mental capacity

Your mental (cognitive) capacity can expand and contract depending on the nature and quantity of information you are processing. How is your thinking impacting your energy levels and your wellbeing?

A recent study concluded that we process more than 6000 thoughts each day – that's 6.5 per minute in our waking hours.[55] We address thousands of assumptions, inferences and beliefs, all at pace. We jump from one unrelated thought to another. It can be exhausting and can impact how you feel in the moment.

I like to think of the brain as a sponge that becomes saturated with thoughts, often to the point where it can no longer absorb any more. It takes some time to wring out the sponge to create space to allow for more thoughts. If this doesn't happen, the additional information will simply wash away.

As a leader you process thoughts resulting from conversations, emails and multimedia from teammates, customers and more. This overlays with the thoughts you are creating based on your own observations of data, to which you attach your assumptions, which form your beliefs.

It doesn't take long for this process to impact your wellbeing. When you have too many thoughts to consider, slow yourself down to allow for an increased attentional focus. Consider what is in your control and what is not so you can identify where to hold your focus. Imagine emptying your thoughts into the buckets pictured in Figure 8 to decide where to invest your cognitive energy.

Notice what kinds of thoughts are soaking your sponge. Negative thoughts can absorb a tremendous amount of energy. One self-coaching strategy I recommend involves pausing to restructure your thinking to gain a new perspective. That small break of time can allow you to open a mental window, offering a breath of fresh air and a new way of viewing an issue. Adopting an open mindset of wonder can make space for the possibilities of what *might* happen next, rather than catastrophising about what *will* happen next.

Ada used this technique of pausing to make some space for herself between meetings. In this time (usually 10 minutes), she would notice her thoughts and consider the impact they were having on her.

She would do some deep breathing to ground herself and would then make a choice as to how to respond.

Figure 8: Buckets of control

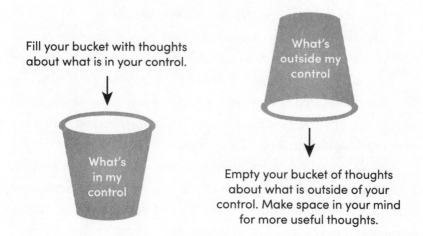

Fill your bucket with thoughts about what is in your control.

What's outside my control

What's in my control

Empty your bucket of thoughts about what is outside of your control. Make space in your mind for more useful thoughts.

Sometimes Ada simply wrote down the actions she needed to take so she could park her thoughts rather than carrying the related cognitions and emotions into her next meeting. If she was upset about a conversation or outcome from the previous interaction, she could use this approach to reduce the emotional and cognitive burden that otherwise would remain. She would then be present to lead into the next unrelated meeting with fewer mental distractions.

Ada told me how, in one instance, in her pause between meetings she noticed her frustration with her colleague. During the ten-minute break she was able to jot down some points to follow up with him later. This didn't solve the issue immediately, but it did allow her to release her frustration and related thinking before stepping into her next meeting. She found she was less distracted and more positively engaged in that meeting as a result.

Consider deliberately scheduling a break or a pause between interactions with others to release your cognitive burden and free up your energy for the next task at hand.

Spiritual capacity

This section of the chapter is not focused on religious considerations; rather, it's about what gives you meaning in what you do. What purpose did you identify in Practice 1? What impact do you want to create? What's the next best step for you to take today?

Understanding how your actions align with your purpose provides a source of motivation, determination and endurance that can energise you. Just thinking about what engages or excites you can create a renewed energy source to carry you forward. Similarly, considering why you matter and are of value provides you with a key inner resource that fuels positive responses to life challenges.[56]

Making some space for reflection and renewal is important. Incorporate a ritual of regularly reviewing your purpose against what you are engaging with at work. Remind yourself of your values, meaning and purpose and how the outcome of your work is aligned.

Attending to your energy levels

The action of attending to your energy levels is where self-coaching really comes into play. The following self-coaching exercise asks you to consider some rituals and habits to support each of the four areas of capacity: physical, emotional, mental and spiritual.

Self-coaching exercise

Review the sample ritual template in Table 5. Copy the table into your notebook, and fill it in for your own situation. Note what your new rituals or habits might be, and list the corresponding actions that will support you in establishing and maintaining the ritual. Then, put it into action! Keep a copy of the template handy so you can calibrate your success against your new goals.

It takes a bit of time to form new habits. Share your intentions with a colleague or family member so they can support you with these new goals.

Table 5: Sample ritual template

Capacity area	Selected ritual/habit to generate energy	How I will support the ritual
Physical	• Regular exercise in green space: daily 30 minute walk • Nutritious food selection • Eight hours' sleep	• Schedule daily walk in my diary • Choose a healthy lunch and eat it away from my desk • Set an alarm on my phone one hour before planned sleep to allow for wind-down
Emotional	• Complete daily list of my three best things and what went well • Demonstrate gratitude by thanking colleagues for their efforts • Listen to music to prompt an emotional shift • Smile	• Set a reminder on my phone to prompt five minutes of thinking time to complete my lists • Consider team members who have done a good job and email them my thanks • Use my playlist during the day to alter my thinking and related state • Just do it!
Mental	• Utilise my strengths • Reflect on my success, and apply learnings to build my future chance of success • Recovery breaks (five to ten minutes) for each 90 minutes of work where I step away from my desk, stretch and clear my thoughts • Control my time so I can focus my attention on my priorities	• Attach a sticky note to my laptop noting three key strengths, and select one to focus on each day • List recent successes in my notebook or phone for ongoing reflection • Set my alarm to sound every 90 minutes during working hours to remind me to take a physical break from my desk • Schedule meetings to start 10 minutes after the hour to improve control of my time • Block time in my diary to reflect on my progress towards my goals

Capacity area	Selected ritual/habit to generate energy	How I will support the ritual
Spiritual	• Reframe the mundane to support my performance • Recognise which of my values are important to me	• Write down my purpose statement and stick it on my office wall for reference • Reframe my goals to match my purpose and values • Book in annual leave to take a break and re-energise and reframe towards my purpose-driven activities

Working around energy obstacles

There are several common obstacles leaders face that can draw down energy levels. How you notice and respond to each of these obstacles is critical to your ability to manage your energy levels.

Workload and deadlines

My coachees often raise workload and deadlines as energy obstacles in our coaching conversations. As we discussed in Practice 5 the demands on your time, and your ability to influence them, is important to consider. Your use of time represents how your energy is consumed. Asking yourself the questions in the following self-coaching exercise can help you identify how you might alter your time commitments so you can have more control and better manage your stores of energy.

Self-coaching exercise

Self-coach your way through the following questions and listen to your responses. Consider the options that might be available to support you and the actions you can take. Then, make a plan to facilitate change.

Here are the questions to work through:

1. Write down your upcoming deadlines. How critical are the deadlines? Are there any that will be difficult for you to achieve?

What possibilities are there to adjust the deadlines for a more attainable time frame?

2. Who can make this decision? If you are empowered to do so, what is a more reasonable time frame? If you can't make this decision yourself, who holds the power to consider whether a new time frame can be set? When can you contact and seek the support of this person in relation to the deadline? How will you best communicate your concerns so that they are understanding of your circumstances?

3. Where you can't alter the deadline, who can assist you with the work required? Who can you delegate to, and how quickly can you engage them to assist you? Be sure to delegate effectively, giving the person context so they understand the meaning behind the tasks asked of them. This will enable greater engagement and quality of performance. (In Practice 9 we'll talk more about empowering others and effective delegation.)

4. Who might you speak with to access further resources or team members? How can you influence those people to provide additional resources to support you with your deadlines and workload? What factors might be important to address so that they understand your current needs and what you are asking of them? This may include discussing dates, time frames, duration of access to additional resources, the skill sets required and details of the project or task you are working on.

5. Can the scope of work be altered? How might you meet the deadline using an alternative methodology? What is being done that is non-essential to the deliverable yet may be consuming time? How agile can you be in your methodology?

6. What other projects or tasks are consuming your time, and can you re-prioritise these to free up some time to focus on the most important and urgent deliverable? Who can assist with these other tasks to enable you to maintain your focus?

Work-related travel

As glamorous as work-related travel might sound, the reality can involve lots of unproductive time sitting and waiting at airports, on delayed planes and in heavy traffic. Standing in queues for taxis, to board planes and waiting for what seems an eternity at baggage carousels is energy-depleting. Plane travel can also be dehydrating, which exacerbates fatigue. Time zone differences and unfamiliar bedding can interrupt sleep. Early starts and late nights where work is squeezed into the time you have at your location can be physically disruptive. Add to this your concurrent juggling of things back home and it's no wonder you are exhausted. So, what might you do to resolve this fatigue?

One easy solution is to travel less! That may sound fallacious, but consider the time and energy you might save if you could instead meet with people via videoconference. With tools such as Skype for Business, Microsoft Teams and Zoom, it can make much more sense (financially and energy-wise) to collaborate remotely rather than face-to-face. Remote collaboration is also an environmental plus.

When face-to-face meetings are required, consider travelling to your destination the night before rather than commencing your day with a 4 am wake-up call. This is particularly helpful in avoiding possibilities of cancelled early morning flights due to weather or engineering problems, which will add to your stress and require panicked diary reshuffling.

When you're travelling, especially across time zones, make sure you get some sunlight. Sunlight regulates your circadian rhythms and sleep cycles. Pack your sports shoes so you can do some exercise while you're away. This might be a brisk walk or run around the city, or a session in the hotel gym. Even using your hotel room to do stretches, yoga or other forms of exercise can be beneficial. Exercise will get the blood flowing and assist you with managing fatigue.

Think about what you eat and stay hydrated. As tempting as it is to buy takeaway food or indulge in the room service menu or the minibar, consider the impact this will have on your energy. If the food selection will nourish you, go ahead. If it will weigh you down and tire you, consider other options.

Seek support from the hotel. If your room is noisy or has poor bedding, loud air-conditioning or other issues that are keeping you awake, seek assistance from the hotel. Hotel staff will usually be happy to help, but they can't do so unless you bring the problem to their attention. You are paying for a service, so make use of it!

Take your annual leave

I hear too many stories of career-minded folk battling through fatigue with a full book of annual leave yet to be taken. According to Roy Morgan, Australia's paid workforce has more annual leave due than ever before: 185 million days' worth.[57] I have not met anyone who, when fatigued, has not benefited from taking their annual leave. Yet it's often the last thing people think to do to deal with low energy.

Taking a break is a healthy form of self-care. Whether you create a series of long weekends or take a week, a few weeks or more, taking your annual leave allows you to break the circuit and recharge your batteries. Your health benefits immediately, as you'll have time to rejuvenate, refresh, step away from work stress and anxiety, and empower others to stand in your shoes while you do something other than work.

I strongly believe that we have one life to live and we should take care of ourselves in it. During my 30-plus-year professional career I have always ensured that I have taken annual leave each year – and I've experienced no resulting detriment to my career progression. And I've intentionally taken leave to enjoy other aspects of my life. I've travelled overseas and locally, spent summers at home at our beautiful Aussie beaches, and enjoyed time with friends and family and time for me. It's important to live your life and avoid the temptation to work throughout your leave. Let's be honest: when that occurs, it's barely leave; it's just working remotely.

Trust that others can hold the fort while you take a break, just as you do while they take theirs. You wouldn't expect your team members or colleagues to work during their annual leave, so treat yourself equitably and do the same.

Book some leave in. Block your diary. It's called *leave* for a reason: you need to *leave* work behind while you enjoy other pursuits and replenish your energy.

Self-coaching summary

♦ Stop, survive and flourish! It's important to exercise control over how you live your working life.

♦ Develop daily rituals to support your physical, emotional, mental and spiritual energy capacity.

♦ Consider how you can reduce energy depletion by working around obstacles: reviewing workloads and deadlines, planning for work-related travel and taking annual leave.

Practice 7

Building your personal board of directors

Mac became a senior leader at the same time as me. Our leadership journeys followed differing paths; however, I was always curious to understand the speed of promotion and the interesting opportunities that came his way. I navigated my own journey reasonably independently. At times it felt a little lonely, but I was reticent to ask for help. Maybe it was pride: I didn't want people to think I didn't know what to do or how to do it. I wanted them to think I was wise enough and skilled enough to lead my way. Part of it was fear and lack of confidence: I didn't feel comfortable asking for other leaders' help or imposing on them to learn how they had achieved what they did, or whether they could afford me the next opportunity. I also didn't like the thought of putting myself out there and feeling more vulnerable than I needed to. Leadership was hard enough, so why make it harder? I thought my work would speak for itself.

I soon realised this was not the case. As I observed Mac's success, I noticed that he was surrounded by other leaders, and he looked so comfortable with them. He was offered opportunities, canvassed for ideas and regularly teamed up with other leaders. He built a strong relationship with a senior leader who first was his coach, then later his advocate as the relationship matured. He also had a number of mentors who he learnt from. He didn't wait for his work to speak for itself: he spoke to others, and they spoke *of* him. Most people spoke of him positively with good intent, and benefits and opportunities came his way as a result.

In time I realised I could learn from Mac's approach. I engaged with a mentor and coach and started to enjoy the benefits that came with having this support crew. My career opportunities expanded, as did my learnings. I felt a greater sense of belonging and I matured in my leadership. If I had put a support crew in place earlier in my leadership journey, who knows what other experiences I may have encountered? Who knows how much more connected I may have felt?

Finding your support crew

Research suggests that those who engage a coach, mentor or sponsor are much more likely to have success in achieving their goals, be exposed to a greater number of career-related opportunities, build and develop skills, be promoted at a fast rate and receive greater remuneration.[58] Setting yourself up with a team of experienced and effective coaches, mentors and sponsors – your personal board of directors – gives you greater ability to grow and develop, test your ideas, seek advice and receive support and advocacy. This group of support people can team with you to help you understand and work through the unique challenges you face as a leader. Having a support crew greatly reduces feelings of loneliness and builds relatedness.

Knowing the differences between the roles of coach, mentor and sponsor can assist you with gaining the most from these relationships. In simple terms, a mentor *tells*, a coach *asks* and a sponsor *advocates*. This chapter will also help you recognise the role *you* can play to get the most out of each relationship and improve your leadership your way. You will be equipped to self-coach your way to designing your own board of directors.

Mentors

'I just want someone to tell me what I should do!' said Noah. 'I really want some advice about the best way to be promoted.'

What Noah was seeking was a mentor: someone who could offer advice based on their subject matter expertise or their experience stemming from their lived or professional circumstances. Noah wanted someone who could tell him what to do or be highly suggestive in how he could approach his issue.

Mentors are helpful when you are seeking advice or wanting to learn from another's wisdom and experience. They can assist by talking through how they would approach a problem if they were in your shoes. Mentors share their perspective, often through the lens of what has worked for them or by referencing their insights or experience. Their advice reflects their position as an experienced professional who may have worked through a similar predicament in their career, and who draws on their reflections to assist you in solving your problem. The intention is for the mentor to transfer their knowledge to you, allowing for your further growth and learning. They typically tell you their proposed solutions to your challenges.

Research studies have demonstrated the value in engaging a mentor. Promotions and salary increases arise more frequently for those who are mentored compared with those who are not.[59] Interestingly, this outcome also extends to those who act as mentors. They too report improvements to salary, promotion rates and subjective career success than those who have not mentored others.[60] This research supports your transition to become a mentor as your career advances and you lead your way – a future goal to orient yourself towards.

The benefits for mentees are easily defined; they include access to a more senior audience of leaders, opportunities for bigger and higher-profile roles, and the opportunity to receive open and honest feedback in discussion with an experienced leader.[61]

Identifying a mentor

Your relationship with your mentor is critical to how successful the mentoring is. You have an important part to play in increasing the effectiveness of your mentor–mentee relationship. At the outset, think about what you are looking for in a mentor. Is it someone who has experience in your organisation, industry, subject matter or market? Assess what you are hoping to learn from their mentorship. Consider their reputation as a mentor. Have others benefited from their advice? Does this person match what you are seeking from a mentor? Do they have time to invest in you?

I suggest identifying a potential mentor and approaching them for a conversation to help you consider these questions. My experience is that this approach is more successful than having someone arbitrarily appointed as your mentor. Building a relationship with your mentor is a critical part of the mentorship, so investing in a relationship with someone who is of interest to you, rather than someone you feel obliged to create a connection with, is preferable.[62]

I was once appointed a C-suite executive mentor as a part of a leadership program I was participating in. It wasn't someone I identified myself but an appointment. Everyone I spoke to about the opportunity I'd been given raved about how lucky I was and what they would do to be given this chance. I saw things a little differently. I liked and respected the mentor I'd been assigned very much, but I felt a little intimidated by them. I felt I had little autonomy in the appointment and didn't feel that I could be vulnerable within the relationship and connect as required. I didn't feel comfortable talking about some of the issues I was grappling with, as I felt (perhaps unfairly) that I may be judged.

It was a shame, as it could have been a fabulous opportunity to learn from this person; however, the imposter in me got the better of me, and I attended just one session. My self-talk created several untested assumptions that inhibited the ease of forming a mentor–mentee relationship.

I opted out of the proposed relationship and approached a leader I had admired for many years – someone I had teamed up with over time and had an existing relationship with. This was my preferred stance, and it worked wonders.

Creating the relationship

Once you have identified your preferred mentor, the next step is to seek their interest and availability to act as your mentor. Not every prospective mentor has the time to create this relationship. It's better to establish early whether the person you have identified has capacity for the commitment you are after. This takes a conversation where you can formally inquire as to their interest in and availability to mentor you; from there, you can start to dig deeper to assist each other with building your mentor–mentee relationship.

It's important to consider your and your mentor's expectations of the mentoring relationship. Mentoring is unlikely to be highly effective if you simply book a meeting time with your mentor and arrive hoping to learn from their stories! Arriving for your mentoring session without any forethought is not respecting the mentoring relationship. Like you, your mentor has a busy schedule. The relationship will be most effective if they are *working with you* to guide and support you in your leadership journey. If they don't know much about you, how will they know where to direct your thinking? Taking time to understand each other's experience and expectations is critical.

The first session can be used to build rapport and an agreed understanding of what you will both bring to your mentoring sessions. What is their experience of mentoring, and can they advise an approach that has worked for them? What are your hopes for the mentoring relationship? How often will you meet, and who will be responsible for scheduling the meeting dates? Invest in understanding what will work best for you both before you dive in. At this first session, share your goals with your mentor so they understand what you are hoping to achieve. This can assist them with directionally advising you, or even challenging your goals to help you better your opportunities for success.

In the sessions to follow, consider the issues you are grappling with and pose questions or problems to your mentor. Challenge yourself to clearly articulate your topic of concern and help your mentor understand the problem, barrier, hurdle or gap you are faced with. It's also helpful to share your ideas around the issue so the mentor can reflect on how advanced or otherwise you are in finding a solution. Rather than expecting a single-sided lecture from the mentor, offer your thoughts and use questions to clarify your mentor's views to foster a deep conversation. You are hoping to develop a trusted relationship, rather than an information service devoid of any connection.

Reliance on your mentor

I'm often asked whether it's worthwhile engaging in multiple mentor relationships. This is largely a question of time management and personal choice. Those who engage with multiple mentors are likely to enjoy increased job satisfaction and wider networks, yet they may also experience greater conflict due to potential divergent advice stemming from each mentor.[63] Be careful not to have too many solutions on offer from too many mentors, as you may find yourself confused as to what to do.

Also be mindful of over-relying on your mentor. Some mentors relish the idea of solving your problems for you and feeling they have led you to the right outcome. I've witnessed sessions in which a mentor is asked for advice and they offer a solution that worked for them and the nuances of their personality, confidence, experience, relationships and so on. The mentee listens, nodding and smiling as appropriate, then leaves the session thinking, 'No way! That would never work for me!' A problem supposedly solved remains unsolved.

The solutions and advice your mentor offers broadens your perspective on what's possible – how someone else may have solved the problem you are facing. While you may not respond in the same manner as your mentor or take on their solution, you can at least consider their experience and understand how yours differs. The disconnect between your situation (personality, confidence, experience, relationships and so on) and theirs can lead you to a point of reflection. Here you can gain further awareness of what you would like to develop to be further advanced in supporting yourself through the issue at hand. For example, you might identify a need to build your interpersonal confidence, self-confidence and communication skills. You might work on this independently or seek support from your coach.

'So, what does a coach do?' I hear you ask. Let's look at how a coach can support you now.

Coaches

When I was speaking with Noah about his options he questioned the difference between mentors and coaches. 'Aren't they the same thing but with different names?' he asked. 'Don't they both tell me what to do?'

Not at all; they are quite distinct. Remember that a mentor is someone who *tells* you what they think is the solution to your concern or the direction to your goal. Coaching takes an alternative stance. It has been defined as 'unlocking a person's potential to maximise their own performance. It is helping them to *learn* rather than teaching them'.[64]

I like to think of coaching as a collaborative conversation that supports *you* discovering insights that lead to greater success. The discoveries are unearthed through a process of the coach *asking* you for your thoughts. In this way, coaching conversations become a reflective activity through which you can build your self-awareness and develop your understanding of the impact of your behaviours, emotions and thoughts. You become better informed to make choices regarding the impact you wish to have and how your behaviours, emotions and thoughts may or may not support that desired impact.

What I love about coaching is the exploration and discovery that occurs. Rather than me acting as a mentor and *telling* you my suggested solution to your problem, or how *I* think you should achieve your goals, coaching empowers you to support yourself when faced with issues requiring resolution. You learn about yourself, discovering why the issue at hand is important to you, how you feel about it, what meaning you are giving to it and what you can bring of yourself to respond to it.

Coaching allows you to build your skills by practising alternative behaviours, emotions and thinking. It increases your mindful awareness of your effectiveness in responding to the issue at hand. Coaching is generally goal-oriented and can also allow for the development of specific skills – such as communication skills, leadership skills and other skills that may assist you in achieving your goals.

The benefits result from your coach asking you questions, creating a space for your contemplation and discovery. This space is non-judgemental, allowing for your open and honest reflection and assessment of what you may discover. The coach provides a reflective stance to help you hear what they are hearing, what they are *not* hearing, what they are noticing and what patterns are becoming evident through what you are sharing. This helps you to increase your self-awareness and ability to uncover how *you* would like to approach your goals, issues, problems and challenges.

As a result, you discover what might work for you and what might not. These revelations can support you with your current coaching conversations; you can also carry the learnings onwards to support your independent work, since you're not relying on your coach to tell you what to do.

How to get the most out of coaching

There are several things you, as coachee, can do to get the most out of the coaching relationship.

First, be honest with your coach. Coaching is focused on you, not on the coach. Don't feel you need to impress your coach by exaggerating your success or overstating how often you practised your new techniques between coaching sessions. Give your coach feedback about what's working and not working for you in your coaching sessions. Lean into the process of discovery. Try to build rapport and trust with your coach, just as you hope they are doing with you. The sooner this is built, the more valuable and impactful the coaching relationship will be.

It's important to ensure you are open to feedback from your coach. The more open (and less defensive) you are, the more you will learn. Reflect on what you might like to practise to effect change. Understand why you are motivated to change. What is driving you to alter your behaviours, emotions and thinking? Knowing this can support you as you find opportunities to practise between coaching sessions.

Coaching works best when you take away actions to work on in between sessions. Keeping a coaching journal or notebook can help you capture your reflections, actions and progress. Change will not arise if you don't mindfully engage in your new or improved practices. Ask for additional learning sources from the coach, whether it be articles, books, podcasts or TED Talks. All of these can support your learning. Let others know that you are working on changing. When you are aware that others are watching for the change, you are more likely to invest in working on yourself. You know that what you are doing will be noticed, and you can receive feedback regarding the effectiveness of what you are doing.

Make sure you understand the boundaries of coaching. Coaching is not counselling, therapy, mentoring or consulting. Discuss the boundaries of the relationship with your coach so that you understand the expectations of this relationship. Be sure to seek a coaching contract that sets out expectations around confidentiality, ethics, timing, payment, disclosures and other related issues.

Lastly, assess the quality of your coach. Does your coach use an evidence-based coaching practice? Do they carry obvious biases? Is the coach attuned to your agenda or are they addressing theirs? Does the coach challenge and support you, or rescue you by telling you what to do (more like a mentor)?

Sponsors

Coaching and mentoring both play an effective role in your development, but they are not necessarily going to advance you towards new opportunities and promotions. Research shows that men with a sponsor are 23 per cent more likely to gain a promotion than those without, while women are 19 per cent more likely.[65]

A sponsoring or advocacy relationship is based on an understood intention that the sponsor will *proactively* seek to identify opportunities for you. These might be opportunities to showcase your current skills, to develop your skills or relationships or to be recognised for your capabilities and contributions. Sponsorship goes beyond the role of a mentor or coach.

The sponsor's role is to amplify you, bringing you to the attention of others to create further opportunities for your success. These opportunities may allow you to develop your network by engaging with stakeholders with whom you have no current relationship. The sponsor's role is to advocate for and represent you in forums in which you might not otherwise have a voice. For instance, a sponsor may hear of a new piece of work that is being generated for a client. They may recognise that your skills and experience would be relevant to the project and recommend you for the initiative.

Your sponsor must have a detailed understanding of your goals and aspirations so they can recognise relevant opportunities and advocate for your involvement. Their relationships with *their* stakeholders must be sufficiently developed so they can influence these decisions.

Business researchers Julia Taylor Kennedy and Pooja Jain-Link say a sponsor has three primary responsibilities:

> *... to believe in and go out on a limb for their protégé; to use their organizational capital, both publicly and behind closed doors, to push for their protégé's promotion; and to provide their protégé with 'air cover' for risk-taking.*[66]

Your sponsor shields you from critics, enabling you to more easily work on stretch projects and take on greater risk. By recommending you, the sponsor puts *themselves* at reputational risk, so you need to be very mindful of the role you play in ensuring that you deliver as best you can in return.

My preferred way to think of sponsorship or advocacy is that the sponsor should:

- be a *catalyst* (create opportunities for you)
- *champion* you (be your voice when you are not in the room)
- *connect* you (open their network to you).[67]

In building your relationship with your sponsor, it's imperative that you develop rapport and trust so that the sponsor is inspired to bring you into the ring. The sponsor will believe in your value and will work to deliver opportunities that accelerate your career. You'll receive broad exposure to the kinds of complex problems, decision-making and key stakeholders you will likely work with in the future.[68]

What's in it for the sponsor?

Your sponsor should be personally invested in your success. By engaging and developing you through sponsorship they are creating a legacy and building succession plans. They are also supporting themselves in achieving their own success by gaining your assistance towards their own goals and objectives as a part of the sponsoring relationship.

Sponsorship is a two-way relationship, in which you will also support your sponsor by assisting them with special projects requiring discretionary effort or your particular skill sets. You may bring your diversity of skills and thinking to the sponsor, which expands their 'bench of talent', supporting their professional goals and success.[69] Economist and author Sylvia Ann Hewlett refers to this as the 'wind behind the sails of the sponsor'.[70] Those who act as a sponsor are more likely to attain the high-profile assignments, promotions and pay rises they seek, due to the 'sponsor effect'.[71] Hewlett's research demonstrates that men who sponsor are 73 per cent more likely to attain a promotion compared to men who don't act as a sponsor, and women are 50 per cent more likely.[72] The sponsorship role is something you should be cognisant of as you lead your way and look to take on sponsorship of others down the track.

Finding a sponsor

Finding a sponsor is not as easy as choosing a mentor or a coach – typically, a sponsor selects you – but there is no harm in asking if you believe there is potential for a sponsoring relationship. A sponsor will be looking to sponsor someone who is able to contribute to the sponsor's own goals, as well as experiencing success when taking up opportunities and building their network. They want to lessen their risk of sponsoring by selecting high-performers to sponsor. Consistently completing your best work and building your own eminence may bring you to the attention of a potential sponsor.

Consider the opportunities you have to inform others of your impact in a measured way. Remember to be humble – this is not about showboating. It's about recognising suitable opportunities to notify stakeholders of your success.

Consider why it would benefit your stakeholders to be aware of your wins. Is the outcome of your work something that would support *their* goals and future success? Could you assist them with achieving *their* pursuits through the nature of the work or methodologies you adopt? How does the value you bring aid them in *their* initiatives? Frame the delivery of your story in such a way that stakeholders and potential sponsors can identify the potential benefit your contribution makes towards broader pursuits.

A sponsor is unlikely to advocate for you if they don't know of you. Reflect on the relationships you have, and invest in those that might lead to future sponsorship. Collaborating with others is a positive way to establish broader relationships and draw attention to your contribution. Use your creativity, curiosity and problem-solving skills to showcase your abilities. Listen out for projects your potential sponsors are working on and, where appropriate, offer your assistance or unique skills to assist them.

Build trust and loyalty with those you hope will sponsor you. Have quality conversations in which you give of yourself and learn from others. You can demonstrate your loyalty through teamwork, providing honest feedback and supporting others' vision, strategy and goals.

Once you have a sponsor, continue to work hard to maintain the trust in that relationship and be sure to deliver back to your sponsor. Don't take the sponsor for granted, as this is a sure-fire way for the relationship to fizzle out. The benefits of being sponsored can assist you significantly with leading your way, navigating your career and arriving at your chosen (or recommended) destination. Stay alert throughout the journey!

Reverse (reciprocal) mentoring

Reverse (reciprocal) mentoring is a recent trend and another consideration for your personal board of directors. In reverse mentoring, Millennial and Gen Z mentors typically assist digitally ill-equipped senior leaders, improving their understanding of technology and its uses and benefits. Reverse mentor programs connect senior leaders with younger generations, mainly with the objective to learn about artificial intelligence and social media from the digitally astute. The idea is to let the less-experienced employee guide the more experienced, with both benefitting from the arrangement.[73]

As reverse mentoring has become more widespread it has extended beyond technologically driven conversations. Senior leaders can also use reverse mentoring as a tool to assess how they are performing and perceived. A reverse mentoring relationship can provide helpful insights from junior team members around connectivity, engagement and the effectiveness of the leader's communication style, vision and goal approach. The relationship can provide helpful points of reflection where the leader can seek insights into their leadership impact.

Personally, I've found reverse mentoring to be a valuable learning experience and a testbed for improving my leadership impact. It has helped me become cognisant of my effectiveness and provided opportunities to test initiatives with my reverse mentor to establish whether my proposed alternative approaches might resonate with the broader team. My reverse mentor's insights and understanding of the team dynamics was a treasured resource, helping me to reconsider my impact. On one occasion I learnt that what I thought might be an appealing and exciting work initiative was in fact perceived as outdated and a little bland. With this insight I was able to refresh the initiative quickly to better engage my team. The awareness that comes from having a trusted reverse mentor is invaluable. The mentor can provide 'just-in-time' feedback and refreshing honesty and perspective that you may not get in a formalised performance survey such as a 360-degree feedback survey.

As with the relationships described earlier, choosing a reverse mentor requires selecting a colleague who is open to performing in the role, and who sees the benefits of building a closer professional relationship with you that allows for honest feedback and discussion of your leadership. You must bring psychological safety to the relationship so the team member does not feel at risk when they're sharing challenging feedback with you – keeping in mind you're a senior colleague who has the ability to impact their career experience. In return you can mentor that person through their own career journey. Both of you will become better equipped to lead your way.

Self-coaching exercise

Complete Table 6 to identify your own professional board of directors. Assess the diversity of the experience of your selected members and ask yourself why you want to engage with them. What is the reason for their selection?

Finally, consider what you want out of each relationship and how you will determine their success. This can be a useful point of reference in your ongoing assessment of those selected to support you.

Table 6: Your personal board of directors

	Name	Position/ title/area of expertise	Reason for selection	How will you determine whether this relationship is successful?
Mentor				
Coach				
Sponsor				
Reverse mentor				

Self-coaching summary

♦ Build your own board of directors (a mentor, a coach, a sponsor and a reverse mentor) to support your growth and development, test your ideas, seek advice and opportunities, and have someone advocating for you.

♦ People with a coach, mentor and sponsor more readily achieve promotions, salary increases and career opportunities compared with those who don't engage with such support.

♦ A mentor (and reverse mentor) will *tell* you what to do, sharing their wisdom and experience.

♦ A coach will *ask* you questions to help you broaden your perspective, supporting you in advancing towards your goals.

♦ A sponsor will *advocate* for you: acting as a catalyst for opportunities, championing you when you're not in the room and connecting you with their network.

♦ Regularly assess your board of directors to determine whether their appointment remains valuable and effective.

Practice 8

Exploring your leadership impact

Ali, a team leader, arrived back in the office after attending a meeting. His team members noticed his arrival and immediately began to observe his body language, listening for Ali's tone of voice and other signals that might suggest his mood. Ali, talking animatedly on his phone, navigated his way across the room to his office and closed the door without engaging with his team members. All eyes and ears were zoomed in on Ali as his team members processed their perception of his mood. Each frown, rapid footstep and bead of perspiration on Ali's forehead presented a picture to his team members – perhaps of stress, disappointment or concern.

Whether or not Ali's team members' perceptions would hold true remained to be determined, but many quickly adopted a point of view. Some decided it was not the time to approach Ali with a question they had, or to raise an issue or share an idea. It would be a career-limiting move to draw other issues to Ali's attention in that moment. It was better to avoid Ali, as he seemed to be in a negative state of mind.

Ali habitually spent long hours at work, sending emails to teammates late at night. He called his team members into last-minute meetings, giving them little context around the purpose or intent of the meeting. He delegated rapidly and often shared important pieces of information at sporadic times as they came to mind. Ali carried a hefty workload, which gave him little time to spend with his family or friends. He appeared exhausted from the weight of his workload, yet powered on all the same. In fact, Ali overshared about how exhausted he was, the stress he was under, his large workload and his concerns about the organisation.

The ripple effect of this was swift. Like a pebble skimming a pool of water, the team quickly adjusted to what they believed was the mood and accepted work practices. The contagion of Ali's inferred negative emotional state moved quickly across the group, infecting each team member with perceived tension.

Over time, as Ali's patterns of behaviour continued, engagement and motivation within his team began to lapse. The team mirrored Ali's perceived mood. They held back on ideating, collaborating and engaging in a shared flow of information. They didn't want to rock the boat, so they stayed out of Ali's way, interacting only when called upon. Work was not a fun place to be.

On another floor in the same organisation, a team leader, Jo, arrived back from a meeting and greeted her team members as she entered the office. She shared a smile, even though she appeared busy and deep in serious conversation, and acknowledged her teammates with eye contact, a nod of the head and a brief wave hello as she passed. Her team members' heads and eyes were raised as Jo walked past. Although Jo appeared to be busy and under pressure, her demeanour suggested it would be okay to approach her with an idea, concern or question once she was off the phone.

Jo carried a hefty workload, yet she involved her team in work assignments, selecting relevant team members to assist based on their availability and strengths, and made them feel that they mattered. Although Jo had plenty on her plate, she spoke with positive intent about how she would tackle the load. She shared the content and purpose of any assignments she delegated, ensuring completeness of information and setting milestones, check-ins and deadlines. Jo collaborated with other teams to access additional support when her team was reaching capacity. She tried her best to negotiate deadlines with customers and, where possible, set realistic time frames. She understood the importance of work–life balance and wellbeing.

The ripple effect of Jo's positive emotional state carried across the broader team. Jo's teammates responded positively and were comfortable raising ideas and suggestions. They offered to assist and extended themselves with discretionary effort and new ideas. The atmosphere was conducive to collaboration, and people brought their best selves to work.

In both these situations, the truth of the leader's state of mind has not been determined. Yet their leadership shadow doesn't seek the truth. It simply paints a picture of the behaviours and emotions that are presented. And, as they say, a picture paints 1000 words!

Knowing this can help you to consider the leadership impact you would prefer to have with your team – one that creates concern and disengagement, or one that creates positivity and engagement. You can influence the likely outcome.

What type of leader makes a lasting impact?

Leadership is about people – yet too few leaders consider how they impact their team members.

Leaders like you – who focus on leading yourself positively – are advantaged when leading others. You make a difference in our world. You understand the importance of creating a positive leadership experience for those around you, and this transforms people's day-to-day experience. You help others feel valued, effective, worthwhile, connected and respected. You improve your own wellbeing and that of others. You make the world a better place.

Leading as your best self when leading others requires continued self-coaching. You must reflect on how you are leading when you're engaging with others, and how you are developing your leadership impact to be positive and long lasting in your absence. Being cognisant of your leadership style will help you discern the impact you are having. Self-awareness will help you lead your way.

The more senior a leader you are, the longer the leadership shadow you cast. In other words, the more senior you are, the more others notice and respond to your actions, behaviours, emotions and thoughts. Role modelling positive leadership can shape your organisational culture, your team's engagement, the discretionary effort team members contribute and the quality of the resulting outcomes.

It's important to have an accurate self-concept to understand what you need to pay attention to as a leader. This helps you make choices to ensure that your intention matches your impact. Developing an accurate self-concept allows you to:

- identify if there is a need to shift your behaviour
- clarify and identify your and others' values
- determine how you motivate others
- set and review goals in relation to your leadership impact.

Sometimes, you simply have to stop to notice.

Noticing your leadership impact

I recently had what I called a crappy day at work. I experienced two situations in which facts were misunderstood, causing tension for me and two others in separate occurrences.

I was frustrated by both situations as neither had resulted in outcomes I hoped for or anticipated. What I did notice was that I was the common denominator in both situations. This made me pause. Which parts of me did I bring to work that day that were helping me, and which parts were hindering? What unintentional impact was I having?

I stepped away from my laptop and sat down with a coffee to reflect on what was going on. I recognised that I work at pace and like efficiency. I am enthusiastic about the projects I am involved in and this can speed up my thinking, sometimes reducing my capacity for tolerance of a slower-paced approach. I also take great pride in my work and the quality of the services I provide, and this focus can leave me frustrated if I am mismatched with a team member who has a lower level of concern.

By recognising how I was impacting my engagement in these two unrelated instances, I was able to process how I could lead my way through each. I could hold myself accountable to alter those behaviours, emotions and thoughts that were not helping my collaboration with others and dial up those that were.

Rather than focusing on what the other people were doing, I used self-reflection to consider what *I* could shift and control to more positively engage and have a more effective impact. I thought about how I could better lead my way. In so doing I increased the quality of my communication and focus to improve the ongoing interactions – and it worked.

Use the four lenses pictured in Figure 9 to critique your leadership effectiveness. Consider each lens and analyse whether your impact on others is positive or negative. Is that impact likely to endure in your absence?

Figure 9: Four lenses of leadership impact

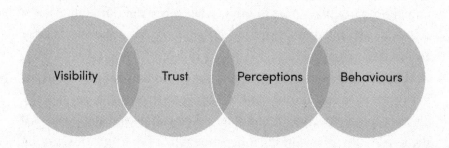

Visibility

What does your team observe in you, and how consistent are your behaviours? If you say one thing but act in a different way, that is sure to be noticed. For instance, if you ask your team to work with urgency to complete a report, yet delay your review of the report unnecessarily, your inconsistent messaging is likely to be noticed and build resentment within your team. Similarly, if you speak of inclusion, yet don't take steps to address others' non-inclusive behaviours, your team members are likely to question your authenticity.

What are your team members observing in you day-to-day? How do you show up?

My coachee Janelle wanted to increase her followership. We discussed how she worked with her team. She said that when she was working in the office, she chose to locate herself in an office with the door closed, at a bit of a distance from where her team sat. She preferred this office as she could get her work done and she felt comfortable in the space. Janelle had told her team members that they could drop by should they need her assistance; but she sat with her back to the glass door, so she rarely observed her team members working behind her and they also had little view of what she was doing.

We discussed the optics of this choice. Janelle felt a lot of warmth for her team; however, her lack of visibility created a chasm between her and its members. They were unable to observe her actions or learn from her interactions with others. They couldn't hear her speak to her customers or colleagues and learn from her conversations. They had to make a particular effort to walk to her office each time they had a question, which led to frustration if they discovered she was busy or away from her desk.

Janelle's lack of in-office visibility suggested that she didn't care for her teammates and didn't want to engage with them. It put her at a distance, placed barriers around her relationships and suggested that she would rather be working independently of her team. This, in fact, was not her truth. She simply had a lot to get done and worked most effectively in a quiet space.

Her team members started to build their followership towards another leader, who appeared present and active in the business. They saw this other leader as a business builder who created opportunities for his team to grow and develop. This leader *appeared* to be more visible. He spent his time in an office next to the team, with the door open when he was not on the phone, suggesting he was more accessible to the team members.

Janelle was struck when I helped her realise how appearances can alter team members' perceptions of leadership effectiveness. She hadn't stopped to self-reflect on what others saw of her and whether this matched her intended leadership impact. She felt that by coming into the office each day she was visible to her team and was making herself accessible. Her team members saw a different picture: Janelle lacked visibility, which reduced her connection with her team.

Consider how you are making yourself visible to your team. What are you doing to create a presence where your team members can see and feel your impact? How are you seen in the workplace – whether virtually or in person?

When your team members can see where you are navigating them to, they will find it easier to follow you. If they don't see you in action and you lack visibility, they may lose confidence in you as their leader. They want to be inspired and motivated by observing your actions. Your visibility in virtual and real terms assists with achieving this.

Embrace technology

Visibility isn't only about your in-person actions; it can also be achieved though the use of technology. This is particularly so if you have some team members working remotely.

Social media is an effective tool to share thought leadership around particular leadership-related issues. Sites such as LinkedIn and Twitter allow you to build eminence in the broader business community. You can use these sites to proactively engage and share your point of view, and inspire not only those in your broader network but your team members.

Intranets and other collaboration tools provide further opportunities to engage with your team members and the wider business. You can share recognition, news, awards and updates. Your team members can also engage with you and see your responses if you utilise comments or 'likes' on their posts.

I've always enjoyed watching the short video messages my CEOs have shared, particularly those of Deloitte Australia CEO Adam Powick. By making himself visible through video, Adam brings himself into the office and his team members' homes. We can see him in his current location, whether that be on the road to visit a client, in his office or at his home. He shares videos of himself wearing casual clothes as well as more formal business attire. His videos make him more relatable; his teams see him as someone who too wears a fleece on a cold Melbourne day. His dog has starred in some of his videos, again letting his team see more of who he is and what he also cares about. He's juggled cricket balls and hit golf balls on video, showing his broader interests and sharing how he maintains his enjoyment of sports. His expressive face communicates what he cares about, as he shares important and critical messages and, as appropriate, jokes and stories that express his character. The video messages amplify his visibility and allow us to develop a deeper connection. We see an authentic, transparent leader who has the courage to be himself and lead as his whole self.

Consider how you can embrace technology to enhance your visibility. If technology is not your thing, find someone who can support you (perhaps your reverse mentor, as detailed in Practice 7). It's better to work through this obstacle than restrict your leadership visibility due to your concerns about your technological skills.

Be seen when things get tough

Remaining present during tough times is essential if you want to inspire, support and motivate your team. Leaders who are seen to take accountability and responsibility to resolve problems are respected and appreciated. Your presence will be noticed and your manner and approach observed. You are more likely to create hope and confidence in your team members if you face challenges head on by their sides.

You can display empathy and compassion and lead your team with kindness as you move to improve the outcome. If you do this, your human-centred approach to leadership will have a positive and enduring impact.

Self-coaching exercise

Reflect on what your team may see in you by responding to the following questions in your notebook:

- Where does your team see you?
- How often do they see you?
- What types of interactions do they observe you in?
- Who do they see you with? Who do they see you avoiding?
- How does this represent you as a leader?
- How consistent is your visibility?
- What needs to be more visible, and how do you plan to enact it?
- How might you dial up your visibility using technology?
- How might you dial up your in-person visibility?

Make a note of any behaviours that require your attention to improve your visibility.

Trust

A trusted leader builds strong relationships with those they lead and work with. It sounds simple, doesn't it? You may be thinking, of course people should trust me! Why wouldn't they? However, gaining people's trust is often more challenging than you might think.

Trust can take time and effort to build and maintain, yet it can be lost in a heartbeat. Trust can be breached with an offhand comment; failure to share credit; thoughtless, rushed communication; and continued unexplained cancellation of meetings. Often the breach is unintended, yet it can take much effort to repair it.

What should you focus on to build trust? Through my coaching I developed the trust hexagon pictured in Figure 10, which demonstrates that to build trust you should focus on developing 'chaver' attributes (consistent, honest, attentive, vulnerable, enabling and responsive). The word 'chaver' originates from Hebrew and means associate, colleague or friend. It's derived from the verb that means 'to join together, to connect'. It hints that the joining or connecting is done out of choice – willingly, through trust.

Figure 10: The 'chaver' trust hexagon

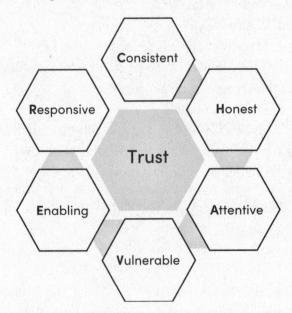

Let's take a look at each attribute in the trust hexagon.

Consistent

Demonstrate consistency in how you treat people: with respect, kindness, interest and openness. Don't give people the cold shoulder when other 'more interesting' people enter the room. Be inclusive and active in engaging with people so they feel at ease in your company.

Listen to your language to be sure that it is consistent with your actions. Do you say one thing yet do another? Ensure that you are dependable and reliable in delivering your promises to demonstrate integrity, quality and value. Make sure you can be trusted to deliver consistently.

Honest

Transparency and honesty in relationships creates trust. Don't over-promise or talk yourself up beyond what you can realistically deliver. Don't twist the truth, especially when it comes to sharing credit. Your colleagues will lose trust in you if you take credit for work that should be attributed to others. You may believe they won't find out you have taken credit out of turn, but they will – if not now, at some stage in the future. Appropriately recognising and crediting others and being honest about your involvement and contribution creates a high level of trust.

Attentive

Take an interest in people and actively listen. Demonstrate your interest in each interaction. Reframe and reflect, and be responsive to the other person's interests and needs. You may have heard about leaders who are highly trusted because they always make people feel that they matter by giving them their *full* attention when they engage with them. Be like those leaders!

Vulnerable

Recognising your errors or mistakes and taking responsibility, where appropriate, builds trust. Humble leaders who admit they don't have all the answers, and who listen to others with respect, actively build trust.

Enabling

Nurture, encourage and support others to be their best selves. Provide context and meaning when you're delegating and empowering others; this removes suspicion and doubt. Help facilitate and create opportunities for others to build skills, grow and develop. Once your team notices that your intention is to coach them to be their best, trust will likely increase.

Responsive

Ensure that you respond to calls, emails, texts, invitations and so on, and do so in a timely way. Demonstrate your interest. Silence can be a relationship killer.

My coachee Simon wondered why he was struggling to build trust with his colleague. When we examined the situation together, we identified that his patterns of communication destroyed trust. He tended not to acknowledge any form of communication, be it a voicemail, email or text. He convinced himself he had valid reasons for not responding; but that was the problem: he had only convinced *himself*. His lack of responsiveness meant he had not shared his reasoning with his colleague, and the continued pattern of non-responsiveness had eroded trust. The relationship appeared to be entirely one-way.

Don't expect the other party to mindread. Unless you communicate with them, they won't realise you are flat out with other urgent deadlines or are out of town, on holiday or otherwise uncontactable. Set up out-of-office responses to support yourself and your relationships, noting when you will be back at work. When you lack time to attend to a stakeholder, send a short response acknowledging their communication and suggest when you will be better placed to respond in detail. Sometimes even responding with 'thanks' or 'noted' can be enough to acknowledge another person. This is so much better than ghosting them – an absolute relationship killer.

Self-coaching exercise

Review the 'chaver' trust hexagon in Figure 10 and select two to three of the attributes to focus on. Identify steps you can take to improve in those attributes, and add them to your weekly reflection to ensure that you are advancing and improving your impact. Once you have improved, select additional attributes from the hexagon.

If you are really wanting to make a change, share your focus with a trusted colleague or friend and explain what you are trying to develop. When you know that others are watching you for change, you are more likely to work towards it.

Perceptions

Perceptions can be hard to change. It can take considerable energy to alter them, especially if they are negative and unhelpful – but being mindful of the perception you are creating is essential if you want to lead with impact.

Lieutenant General David Morrison AO, former Chief of the Australian Army and 2016 Australian of the Year, famously stated, 'The standard you walk past is the standard you accept.'[74] Consider this mantra in all you do. Ignoring unacceptable behaviour can foster a negative perception of what is acceptable to you as a leader. Acting in alignment with your values allows you to set the standard of what you expect so that the perceptions of your leadership equate to the reality.

What might others perceive of your leadership impact? How are you consciously influencing this for the better? What do you do that creates a perception of being inclusive? How do you create an environment of psychological safety for team members where they perceive they can participate without fear of failure or humiliation? How do you create a perception that you are focused on bringing out the best in your team members? What opportunities do you create for your teammates, matched with their individual strengths and purpose?

The answers to these questions may best be discovered by seeking feedback from your team. Their insights can assist you in understanding their perceptions of you as a leader – of your actions, behaviours and emotions. Be sure to listen to the feedback so that they feel heard; this will ensure you are perceived as authentic and truly interested. You don't want to flame a fire of poor perception.

Self-coaching exercise

Consider how you might be perceived.

In Practice 1 you identified your key values. How are you honouring those through your leadership? Write down your key values and reflect on whether others would perceive them in you.

Answer the following questions in your notebook:

- What actions can you take to alter or reinforce these perceptions?
- How can you counter poor perceptions? For example, are you perceived as not pulling your weight, not meeting deadlines, not communicating with others or being inconsistent? How can you address this?
- How can you reinforce positive perceptions others have of you? For example, are you perceived as being fair-minded and inclusive, and having integrity and an ethical mindset? What can you do to cement these perceptions?
- What feedback have you received about how you are perceived? Consider the actions you would like to take as a result and plan for their completion.

Behaviours

What are your behaviours telling others? Do your behaviours match your intentions? Are you reflecting and reframing to ensure your behaviours are contributing to your desired leadership impact?

My coachee Jasmine had a habit of looking at her emails during our coaching conversations. We were coaching virtually, and she seemed unaware that I could see her eyes darting across the screen and her hands moving on her keyboard. Her mind drifted to what she was reading, leading to uneasy pauses in our conversation while I waited for her to recalibrate back into what we were discussing. Jasmine's behaviour suggested there were other things she would rather be doing. She was not focused and was not honouring the time we had agreed to share together.

I brought this to Jasmine's attention and shared with her how it made me feel – somewhat uncomfortable, almost as though I was imposing on her time. I asked her to consider how I was feeling, and how it how might make others in her team feel if she was engaging with them in the same way.

Jasmine hadn't been aware of her behaviour or how it might impact others, and she appreciated having this brought to her attention. Her behaviour had sent me a message that didn't match her intention. This feedback gave her the opportunity to reflect and make a choice as to how she would engage with others during virtual meetings.

Self-coaching exercise

Consider how you behave with others and how it may make them feel.

How do you behave when you are under pressure with a lot on your plate? How do you manage your emotions when you engage with others? What message does your body language convey, particularly when you are stressed? A roll of your eyes, a furrowed brow or arms crossed defensively against your chest can send a message to others around you that you wish to shut down communication. Is this your intention?

What behaviours do you demonstrate that encourage teamwork, feedback and collaboration? Do you have open conversations in which you role model listening skills and curiosity? How are you behaving to encourage others to be the best they can be?

Identify three behaviours you would like to reinforce, and three you would like to alter, to improve how you lead your way. Write these in your notebook. What are the consequences of the behaviours you have identified?

Book some time in your diary to regularly reflect on these questions and consider how your behaviours might be influencing your leadership impact. Some of my coachees do this weekly, while others do so monthly.

Self-coaching exercise

Reflect on the four lenses we've discussed in this practice: visibility, trust, perceptions and behaviours. Identify three things you'd like to start doing (or do more) and three things you'd like to stop doing (or do less).

Once you have completed the lists, make a plan to bring them to life.

Self-coaching summary

♦ How you lead determines the leadership shadow you cast.
♦ Mindfully leading your way will improve your leadership impact.
♦ Assessing what you pay attention to will help ensure that your intention matches your leadership impact.
♦ Your leadership effectiveness can be improved by considering the four lenses: visibility, trust, perceptions and behaviours.

Practice 9

Empowering your team

I noticed a pattern of behaviour in Ren after several coaching conversations. Ren had been working tirelessly in his role. He had grown his business both in revenue and team size and was forever working through an ever-growing list of commitments.

From time to time Ren would be flummoxed when a team member handed in their notice. He thought he had created a great place to work and was often surprised by dips in team member engagement. We discovered engagement was particularly low among the senior members of Ren's team.

With Ren's permission I reflected on what I was noticing in his behaviours. Ren had a high level of concern for his team members and wanted the best for them. He truly cared about their wellbeing, and took it upon himself to roll up his sleeves and help when he felt it necessary. The working pace was fast and the load was heavy, and Ren was conscious of the challenges the team was experiencing during the long working hours that resulted.

Ren's approach to the challenge was to rescue his team. Ren would jump in and take work off them to finish himself, sometimes without consultation. He would hurry them off to spend some time at home with their family and friends, and burn the candle himself – taking the lion's share of what needed to be completed in support of others' well-being. Ren believed that, as the leader, this was the right thing to do.

We discussed the high level of empathy Ren exuded. He was caring, considerate and sensitive to what he believed his team members needed. Yet Ren overlooked the unintended consequences that played out.

While Ren thought of himself as a considerate leader, his tendency to help his teammates had an unexpected impact: he discovered his team felt disempowered and like they weren't trusted to complete their work. They felt micromanaged and were not given the satisfaction of completing assignments that had been presented to them. Their ability to learn from their experiences was too often hijacked when Ren decided to jump in. They were frustrated and felt that they weren't consulted or listened to. Ren could now see how he had limited the team's potential and curtailed opportunities.

I suggested to Ren that he was not supporting or empowering his team members but rescuing them. Ren was standing in his teammates' shoes, tying up the laces and walking with them, rather than inspiring them to walk in their own shoes. I asked Ren to consider standing in his team members' shoes for just a short moment to notice what they were experiencing, before stepping out and supporting them from the sidelines instead. If he could empower his team members to pursue opportunities that would further their skills and development, this would result in improved performance, engagement and motivation.

Ren was quick to respond, wanting to explore how he could lead his way to empower others more effectively. We started with a discussion around what it means to empower others, which I'd like to share with you as another self-coaching strategy.

What does it mean to empower others?

In Practice 3 we explored how self-determination can increase your motivation as a leader. As you lead others, you should consider how you are supporting them in building *their* sense of self-determination. When you pay attention to how you are supporting their *autonomy* (their choices and control over how they work), *competency* (their mastery, via development opportunities) and *relatedness* (their positive connection with others), you empower them to be at their best.

When people feel empowered, they feel trusted, valued, respected and connected to you as the leader who created opportunities for their growth. They feel that they matter, have been seen and heard and can offer a valuable contribution towards a common purpose. They are of significance. As a result, retention and engagement improve, morale and team culture are more positive, and confidence and productivity increase, as do learning, innovation and collaboration. Your leadership will be most effective when you pay attention to the consequences of how you engage and empower your team members. You must identify the ways in which you empower or restrict your team members so you can then choose to redirect your behaviours as required to improve your leadership impact.

Let's now take a look at *how* you empower others.

Get to know your team members

Empowering your team starts with knowing who they are. I don't mean knowing them by name and where they sit in the hierarchy of your organisation; I mean you must *really* get to know them as people. When you know what your team members are striving towards – what their hopes, dreams and goals look like, which of their strengths could be utilised and what motivates them – you will be better equipped to empower them appropriately. Getting to know your team members is imperative to having a positive leadership impact.

Understanding the whole person allows you to tap into what drives them, how they spend their time and what is important to them in leading their lives, in addition to what they want to achieve in their work. It's important to know about their interests, goals and individual needs that require consideration for them to work as their best selves.

This will help you to reflect on *how* you might empower them, such as by offering flexibility in their work hours or location and the projects they might be assigned, or understanding the tools that will support them in fulfilling their work commitments given their own diversity of experience, background, thinking and wellbeing. These insights can better connect you with your team members, enabling informed and trusted engagement.

This practice is very much in sync with how you empower and lead yourself. By better understanding your values, strengths, purpose, goals and motivating factors, you lead effectively with self-determination. You lead as your best self. Leading others is much the same.

Getting to know your team members requires an investment of time. The return on your investment will be well worth it. Your investment in understanding your team will strengthen your leadership impact. You will move from being a leader by title to a leader united through deep relationships.

Self-coaching exercise

List your team members by name on a page in your notebook and complete the columns listed in Table 7 as best you can. If you have a lack of knowledge regarding your team members, book a short coaching session with them to explore these key elements.

Once you have completed the table, challenge yourself to identify opportunities to support your team members' goals, noting which of their skills these opportunities will strengthen. You can share this with them during your coaching conversations.

Ensure you identify how you will hold yourself accountable to creating these opportunities. Maintaining the information in a spreadsheet may aid you in reviewing it from time to time to keep yourself on track. Diarising a monthly review of your progress may also be a useful technique to hold yourself accountable.

Table 7: Getting to know your team members – example

Name	Key values and interests	Strengths	Goals and what matters to them	Opportunities I can create this month	Skills to be developed
Robert Tennetti	Values: • Family (Dad to preschooler) • Social justice and altruism • Affiliation Interests: • Bush regeneration club • Kayaking • Environmental conservation	Strong communicator Attention to detail Networking Environmental education	Promotion to Senior Manager (December) Advisory board member (not for profit) Eminence in climate change Picking up son from school	Lead project delivery for Client X Presentation at climate and sustainability industry event (November) Flexible working hours to support family dynamics	Strategic big-picture thinking Stakeholder influence and management

Show them the way

Motivating your people to work towards common goals is an essential element of positive leadership. When you articulate your goals to your team members, they become better informed as to where you are navigating to. Your leadership plans are visible and your team members can make informed decisions about the way in which they follow you towards their achievement. They can more easily identify opportunities to develop with you, becoming more empowered with these insights. They will have the impetus to participate and be directionally aligned with you in pursuit of the team's common purpose.

Self-coaching exercise

Meet with your team and share the goal hierarchy you developed in Practice 2. Share your purpose and explain the human problem that matters to you and how your team members can contribute to solving it. Communicate how they are significant in resolving the issue. Show them why they matter.

Once your team members understand your goal hierarchy, highlight the areas in which you need support and seek their interest. This allows team members to understand the opportunities available to support the team goals. It helps them see that they are valued and bring value. They can shape their development in line with yours so that you travel as one with a common purpose. They can take accountability for the sub-goals you have highlighted, and they feel like they matter. They will feel significant, of worth, and feel a greater sense of purpose and belonging.

Be on the lookout for opportunities

You develop as a leader when you learn to support others, rather than simply focusing on your own success. In fact, you are more likely to experience success when your team members do. I like to refer to this as thinking of *we*, not just *me*. Identifying projects that allow your team members to build skills not only helps them and strengthens the overall team but strengthens you as a leader.

Demonstrate your faith in others by presenting opportunities and offers of support. Seek insights from your team members regarding the support they need from you or others, the time frames and dead-lines being set and the resources they have access to. Be sure not to throw them an opportunity and turn away. Be available for them to consult with so they feel well supported by you. Check in with them to ensure that they feel equipped to lean into the challenge, and that they are comfortable being uncomfortable as they further learn their craft. Simply knowing that you are aligned with their success builds trust and furthers your leadership impact. These small acts empower your team.

As we discussed earlier in the example with Ren, be mindful that you're showing support rather than jumping in to rescue your team-mates. You can quickly derail their empowerment if you take over without consultation or sufficient explanation. Stand back and allow your team member to do things differently to you; if you have helped them understand the context of the task at hand and the intended outcome, they will most likely achieve success, even if they go about it in a different way to you.

Help them with their mindset

When people feel confident, they are more likely to feel positively empowered rather than empowered with a high risk of failure. Help your team members build their self-determination by asking them questions that focus on each element:

- *Autonomy (choices)* – 'Tell me about how you plan to approach this project. What do you have in mind?'
- *Competency (development)* – 'What are the key technical elements you think are relevant? What methodology might you use in solving this problem?'

- *Relatedness (connectedness)* – 'Who do you need to help you solve this problem? Which team members do you want to support you?'

Short conversations with those you empower can help build their confidence and growth mindset towards what is possible with them at the helm.

Why aren't you delegating?

Once you have completed the exercises in this practice, it's time to review your approach to delegation. As we discussed in Practice 5, not only does effective delegation empower your teammates but it's also a tactical play for you to become less busy. Many people hesitate to delegate when they are busy, suggesting they don't have time to do so. 'How can I delegate? I have no time to tell anyone what I need; it's quicker to do it myself.' However, with some discipline, the time you allocate to effective delegation will win you back additional time to devote to other priorities.[75]

If you habitually resist delegating, be honest with yourself about why. Refer to the common reasons others cite in Table 8. Notice which you relate to so you can identify opportunities to alter your cognitions to more effectively delegate, refocusing your time where it can be best spent.

Table 8: Why I don't delegate

Why I don't delegate	Why I should delegate
It will be faster if I do it myself.	That might be the case, but how many other things do you have to do? What is stopping you from doing them? How will you further develop and empower your team if you don't allow them the opportunity to engage and learn through your delegation? Pursuing the work yourself and avoiding delegation will leave you in a never-ending cycle of increased workload.

Why I don't delegate	Why I should delegate
I don't have team members to delegate to.	This can be a challenge. However, it gives you a chance to engage your curiosity and creativity to establish who might be available to assist you. Consider your stakeholder network and inquire about the availability of people from other teams to support you. Perhaps their team members have related skills that you could utilise. Consider whether you can automate some tasks, creating more time for team members to engage in other work. This might create more space for the value-adding work you do and for more strategic delegation to your team members. If you are consistently under-resourced, consider presenting a business case to recruit and expand your team. Who do you need to bring this to the attention of, and how can you secure their agreement?
My team members don't have the skills to assist me.	Your team members will never have the skills to assist you if you don't coach and mentor them and give them opportunities to develop. You'll always be too busy if you don't build your team members' skills and allow them to support you. You will also reinforce a barrier for your own professional development if you adopt this viewpoint. By failing to coach and mentor team members, you will be less likely to build a high-performing team and more likely to find yourself even busier, responding to disengagement, low morale and poor team behaviours.
My boss asked me to do this.	That might be the case, but you can use your judgement to consider whether your boss's request was in relation to creating an outcome or your *personal* subject matter expertise. If it was the former, you can delegate the task to your team and empower and support them in its completion through quality review and direction. You can still deliver the outcome as requested, together with your team members' insights.
I don't trust my team to do the task.	That's concerning and provides a great opportunity for reflection. Why don't you trust your team members? How can you go about building or rebuilding trust? High-performing teams require trust, so this is a critical issue for you to address.

Why I don't delegate	Why I should delegate
My team is too busy.	They may well be busy, but be careful about making decisions based on this assumption. People are motivated by different factors. Some may be motivated to engage in your task and may be able to 'make room' or use their 'discretionary time' to assist you. They may be able to gain efficiencies elsewhere to benefit from the opportunity to learn from this experience. Allow them the chance to assess their possibility of doing so and give them autonomy over their own time. Assuming that your team is too busy to assist you may be misread as you not offering interesting opportunities for their development. Where you act without discussing your team members' availability, you may be perceived as not trusting them or disempowering them – even if you believe you are being empathetic by not burdening them with additional work. A simple solution is to ask before you conclude that your people are too busy.
I love this part of my job.	That may be true – for now – but consider the possible opportunities you may be missing out on if you hold yourself hostage to this task. Channel your enthusiasm for this task to motivate those around you and notice the ripple effect of your positive emotions on those you delegate to. Free yourself up to experience new things that may also energise you. Importantly, allow your team to grow and feel empowered to do something new.
I'd rather not.	Why? Are you harbouring a fear that is undermining your attitude? Reflect on what you are worried about. Is it that they might do a better job than you? (Wouldn't it be great to lead such an awesome team?) Might you be left with nothing to do and be out of a job? (Do you really want to do the same thing forever?) Do you worry you may lose control? (Think about how you communicate the task to ensure that you remain engaged.) Focus on what is holding you back from delegating and empowering others and challenge yourself to have a more positive leadership impact.

Why I don't delegate	Why I should delegate
It would be unreasonable to ask for help given the short deadline.	Some people love to work under pressure and are at their best when they are working with a sense of urgency towards what may seem like a crazy deadline. Others may like that the time frame is short as they can fit the task around their other commitments. Ask the question and allow them to assess whether they have the capacity to act, rather than holding assumptions about their interest or ability to be elastic with their time management. Empower them to make decisions around their time.

Self-coaching exercise

Review Table 8 and identify the thinking that sounds like you. Write it in your notebook and challenge yourself to overcome your rationales.

Effective delegation

Effective delegation requires the communication of work tasks and desired work objectives; this is very important in enabling team members to apply their skills. Drawing attention to the value and applicability of their competencies helps them feel capable of achieving the desired outcomes. What follows is a sense of calm, confidence and increased resilience.

How can you delegate most effectively? By doing so with purpose and intent. Provide context to those you are delegating to so that they can gain a deep understanding of *why* they have been asked to do certain tasks, as well as *what* they have been asked to do and *how* to do so. This gives greater meaning to the tasks, increasing engagement and avoiding a procedural approach devoid of strategy.

Purposeful delegation can give the most straightforward task more meaning, increasing the connection the person being asked to complete it feels with it. It encourages ownership of and accountability to the task, giving the team member a renewed sense of responsibility to achieve its purpose.

For instance, you could delegate by email in the following way:

Marc, following our meeting with Client X yesterday I'd like you to update the report by Wednesday using the new data attached to this email. Thanks.

This form of delegation will result in a poorer-quality outcome than if you provide context around *why* the person is being asked to perform the request. As a result, the person's response may not be timely or in line with the intuitive mindset you were hoping they would adopt. When you review their work, you might spend more time fixing errors than you anticipated.

You may reframe this delegation to something like this:

Marc, now that we've had that meeting with Client X, we have a better understanding of why they need us to provide more insights in the report. The new data we now have can be used to substantiate their high-risk technical position. We need to be sure to use our skills to draw out the key information and insights from this additional data, rather than simply re-populating the tables in the report. I'd appreciate your help in updating the report by Wednesday, including these new client insights, to better reflect the client's position. Your analytical strengths will be of benefit in ensuring a comprehensive report. Thanks.

This purposeful explanation, which only takes a few extra minutes to share, provides greater context and meaning to the task, in addition to highlighting which of the team member's strengths will be of support. You will have made them feel relevant and that they matter. This approach improves the team member's engagement and, therefore, performance and quality. Your effective delegation has just bought you back some time!

Bringing purpose and context into your delegation brings your team to life. It reminds your team members *why* they are doing what they are doing, helping them find meaning in their contribution to the end outcome. Purposeful delegation is like a power pack that brings connection and energy even to mundane tasks. Without purpose and context, delegation is highly transactional and devoid of meaning, which only reduces people's motivation to engage.

Ensuring the context is understood

When you're delegating it's important to confirm that the team member is left on the same page as you. How often do you think you've completed a comprehensive delegation only to find out later that the team member hasn't heard or understood half of what you said, nor created any notes to reference? Help yourself and save future time by asking the person you're delegating to to take some notes to ensure you are on the same page, and then have them repeat back the key points from the conversation to ensure you have provided sufficient detail. This is your chance to consider whether your communication was confusing, overwhelming, selective or incomplete. You can take a few minutes to reset and fill in the blanks or answer the team member's questions. If you've explained your intention to delegate and empower them, the team member will be better placed to approach the conversation with a common purpose and understand your expectations.

Share gratitude

Once you have empowered others and they've completed the task, showing gratitude for their involvement allows for recognition of their contribution. It's also more likely that they will respond positively when offered opportunities to be involved again. Impactful leaders recognise their team members' contributions and express gratitude in a sincere and authentic way.

As we discussed in Practice 6, gratitude is a powerful positive psychology intervention. It increases positive emotion and contributes to improved performance, job satisfaction and engagement.[76]

Team members who value recognition will feel supported by a leader who provides it. The benefits also extend to you: expressing gratitude increases your positive emotion and improves your wellbeing.

Expressing gratitude may be challenging for you if you are someone who does not personally seek recognition. However, your team members may feel overlooked or taken for granted if you fail to provide them with recognition for their contributions.

As you lead others, you can provide rich feedback regarding their contribution. Consider the different mediums you can utilise, such as email, team social media sites, team meetings, face-to-face praise overheard by others, nominations for awards and so on. If you send an email of thanks directly to the person, CC the person they report to (if this isn't you) so their positive contribution is more widely understood.

Be conscious of your messaging when you're expressing gratitude. A simple 'Thanks, you did a great job!' doesn't provide context around what they did well, and may cause them to question your sincerity. Be specific and articulate what you are grateful for; for instance: 'Thanks for your efforts. I was impressed with your report writing. The messages were clearly articulated, and we can readily understand the actions we need to adopt. Great job!'

It can take some practise and discipline to get this right, but it's an easy way to support your team's wellbeing. They will feel not only empowered but also appreciated and valued. They will feel like they matter and are of significance.

Self-coaching exercise

List the names of those team members you have delegated to during the last month in your notebook. Circle their name if they have supported you or your team to achieve a common goal. Underline their name if they have contributed something that is worthy of thanks. Select a medium to share your gratitude and tick their name off your list once you have done so.

Now that you've completed this task, reflect on how you feel. It's likely that you will feel positive and possibly energised. Keep this in mind for the future as a way of supporting yourself to lead others as your best self.

Block some time in your diary each month to repeat this exercise. The benefits for you and your team members make it worth your time.

Self-coaching summary

♦ Empowering others increases your ability to have a positive leadership impact.

♦ Get to know your team as individuals so you can identify suitable opportunities to engage them in.

♦ Empowering your team increases their self-determination.

♦ Help those you empower to build a confident mindset by understanding how they will use their autonomy, competency and relatedness in fulfilling what they have been empowered to do.

♦ Delegate, delegate, delegate! This is necessary to empower others.

♦ Express gratitude to those you have empowered and who have contributed positively.

Practice 10

The best leaders listen

'So, how did it make you feel?' I asked Ji. Ji paused to contemplate, shuffling in their chair. 'I felt so uncomfortable. I really felt like I was imposing on his time. It was like I didn't matter. I felt awkward and of little value, and I wanted to hurry through what I needed to say so I could leave as quickly as possible.'

Ji had arrived at our coaching session wanting to discuss an interaction they had had with another senior leader. They were feeling unsettled about the outcome of this meeting, as it was an important opportunity to try to influence this leader towards collaborating with Ji.

'It really took me by surprise, as it altered the dynamics of our conversation. I had arrived positively minded and ready to engage in some persuasive debate; however, he gave me every sign that he wasn't listening. I had to repeat myself a few times and, even then, I felt dismissed by his disjointed responses. It felt like he was on autopilot rather than with me in the conversation.'

Ji had invested much time preparing for the encounter and was at a loss. Ji was a skilled listener, always present and open to hearing others' perspectives. Ji had this expectation of others and was troubled when faced with a leader who clearly wasn't listening.

Listening can be hard for some. When people don't listen, you most certainly notice. You know what it's like to feel that a colleague, friend or family member is just not listening. Maybe you've started to share some thoughts with a colleague and noticed they are not engaged, or they simply talk over you. Maybe your colleague is multitasking as you speak to them and appears distracted by their phone or email. You may have repeated yourself, been cut off and tried again before realising they're just not listening!

When people don't listen you feel like you're not being heard, and you may find yourself jockeying with the person to hold their attention. You might become preoccupied with their mental absence. You may be thinking, 'Will you just *listen*?' or, 'Can you just stop interrupting?' Maybe you raise your voice or change your tone and pause to see if they notice. Maybe, just like Ji, you hurry through what you have to say just to get it over with.

Think about how this makes you feel. Ji felt disrespected and devalued. You may feel frustrated, irritated, confused or maybe even annoyed. You may feel of little value and significance. You may feel that your time is not being appreciated. You might wonder, why bother?

This might cause you to end the conversation, walk away, mentally switch off or disengage. You might feel a change in your emotive state – perhaps of irritation, hopelessness, annoyance or disbelief. You may become preoccupied with the outcome of this conversation and play it over in your head.

You won't note this as an enjoyable interaction. In fact, if anything, you may consider avoiding future conversations with this person. You may be less likely to try to deepen the relationship as your trust in the person may have lessened. You won't be inspired by the way they have engaged – or, rather, by the way they have not engaged at all! The long-lasting impact will be less than positive.

During my career I've worked with hundreds of leaders – CEOs, CFOs, CHROs, CIOs, directors, associate directors, partners, operating unit leaders and other leaders of various titles and responsibilities. Their titles did little to reveal or reflect the quality of their leadership.

The leaders who made the greatest impression on me were those who were skilled listeners. These leaders made me feel like I *mattered* by listening to my contributions. It wasn't that they always agreed with what I said. Rather, they reflected on what I said and furthered our conversations. Most importantly, they were mentally present and engaged in the conversation – whether physically or virtually.

Leaders who listen have the biggest impact. This impact is long lasting even in their absence. They make space for others and build connection. They are open to broadening their perspective by listening to others' points of view and ideas. They become better informed, more knowledgeable and more connected to the breadth of issues that may be impacted by their leadership. They learn what is of importance to their team members, colleagues, clients and customers. They are open to learning and discovery, and recognise that they don't have all the answers. They build their connectivity with others by listening and have a positive impact in doing so.

You can be a leader like this who inspires and motivates, connects and contributes, learns and grows. Let's understand how.

Notice how you are listening

One of my favourite authors, American civil rights activist Maya Angelou, is quoted as saying, 'People will forget what you said, people will forget what you did, but people will never forget how you made them feel.' When you listen, you make people feel valued. Learning to listen is fundamental to inspiring and motivating others.

Knowing what you know about your own response to poor listeners and how they make you feel, why would you allow yourself to become a poor listener when you lead and engage with others? I don't believe you'd intend to be a poor listener. Rather, when you listen poorly, I think you lose consciousness of how you are making people feel. You become too focused on your own immediate needs and lose sight of the benefits of listening.

Being busy

As we discussed in Practice 5, we are all busy and getting busier. Time is of the essence, and stopping to listen requires just that – time. Think about that. Listening takes time, and most people talk about how they are time poor. You don't want to waste time, so you might not stop to listen. You might try to rush through the conversation by selectively listening: listening for what you want to hear and then steering the conversation around that. It might feel as though you're being efficient because you're progressing what you have prioritised. However, selective listening can halt conversations. It means you are bringing your own biases to conversations, which reduces your capacity to expand your perspective.

Cognitive processing

Research demonstrates that you think faster than you speak. People speak at an average of 125 words per minute, yet are likely to mentally process at a faster rate.[77] Your brain has room to be doing other things when people are talking to you, which often means you allow for distracting thoughts or that inner voice to enter the conversation, which gets in the way of listening.

Expertise and eminence

As a subject matter expert, you may be passionate about demonstrating your value to your colleagues and clients. This might mean you enter conversations with *your* agenda and thought leadership front of mind, leaving less space for others' views. After all, isn't that what you are being paid for? Isn't that how you create eminence? As you become more senior, don't people expect to hear more from you?

This perspective pulls you into a *telling* mindset, where you tell your team members and clients what to do because you believe your expertise or experience will be helpful. What you haven't stopped to do is test this out by listening to what people really want or need.

Nor have you broadened your own perspective by opening yourself up to what others may know.

Think about the last meeting you had with a client. Who did most of the talking? For what percentage of the meeting was your voice audible? Try to shift this next time so that the greater percentage of time is dominated by others' voices. Change the focus to learning from the other people in the room, rather than proving your expertise.

Becoming a better listener

The first step in becoming a better listener is to raise your level of consciousness. If you can notice how you are listening, you are more likely to be able to fine-tune your listening and be truly present. Notice whether you have cleared your mind of other distracting thoughts and assumptions to allow for new or renewed insights. If you are juggling lots of other thoughts, you are making little room to hear from others. Quieten the voice within your head. Block out distractions and let go of them to focus on the conversation. Make a choice to listen. You have control over your behaviours, emotions and thoughts. You can choose to listen.

You can sharpen your listening by drawing your attention to others. Bring your awareness to any automatic thoughts you carry – whether they be judgements, assumptions or beliefs – and let these go. Listening to others gives you space to counter these.

Questioning techniques

The best listeners use a variety of questioning techniques to learn from the other person.

Open questions can be used to clarify and gather details. They often include the words 'how', 'what', 'why' or 'explain'. For instance, 'Why do you suggest that this is not possible?' is an open question that elicits the possibility of an informed response. Asking someone,

'How do you think that went?' gives you an opportunity to hear their opinion rather than surmising what they thought.

Closed questions confirm thoughts. They tend to produce 'yes' or 'no' answers. For instance, asking, 'Did you prepare your strategy in-house?' is likely to generate a confirmatory response with little detail.

Asking *probing questions* is a great way to explore and learn more from the other person. Probing questions are 'tell me more' questions that seek further clarification. For instance, you could say, 'How would you enable this? Please tell me more so I can better understand', or, 'What else?' Both are probing questions that allow you to seek clarification and extend your understanding.

Keep probing to ensure that you have made space for the other person to share what they want to share. Prompting them further using probes such as 'go on' or 'tell me more' encourages them to unpack what they want to bring to your attention. It also helps you test assumptions you might be holding, reducing the potential for misunderstanding.

Better yet, give context to your questions to help the other person understand why you have asked. This builds trust and removes doubt and suspicion from your question, and may elicit a richer answer. For instance, rather than simply saying, 'I want to ask you some questions about your accounts', you might say, 'I would like to discuss the planning process for the next financial year. I'm curious to understand what your strategy and financials look like. Do you mind if I ask you some related questions?'

When you describe the *purpose* of your conversation, the other person understands *why* you are interested and they are not left wondering where the questioning is headed. Setting the context first paves the way for your questioning, rather than simply jumping into a series of questions shotgun style. You have built a bridge between you and the other person in the conversation, which creates trust.

Self-coaching exercise

In preparation for your next meeting, note down a few *open* questions to support you in learning more from the person you are meeting with. Also consider how you can also provide some context for your questions.

Set yourself a learning goal

Setting a learning goal can be a helpful way to improve your listening. For instance, this might mean entering a conversation with the goal to learn from the other person, rather than simply presenting your view.

Reflect on what you learnt from the last conversation you had. If you only learnt a little, question whether you were truly listening. This is not simply about noticing what you have learnt that is new to you. Notice what you heard about the other person's point of view, even if their view is aligned with yours. Was their point of view balanced, or was it based on assumptions or bias? Was their point of view informed or judgemental? Was it broad or specific? Did you understand their frame of reference, or were you confused by what they shared?

Learning can arise from hearing new concepts and ideas, as well as having existing ideas confirmed. Even when you're listening to the most ordinary conversations, you can still find something interesting to learn by taking an interest in what the other person is saying.

To be a good listener and achieve your learning goal, it's important to suspend judgement and learn what is important to the other person. Hold back your inner voice, which might be telling you what you expect to hear. Change your mental stance and be open-minded. Adopt a curious and open mindset that doesn't prejudge what the other person is saying. Invest in your sense of curiosity to learn more from them – why they hold a particular point of view or what led to their decision. Unpack their perspective by listening and inquiring.

Harvard academic Jennifer Garvey Berger uses the expression 'listen to learn'.[78] I think it beautifully sums up this important element of listening.

Listen to understand

When you're in conversation, concentrate on what is actually being said, rather than just hearing the words. You might notice that you have heard someone speak yet you can't recall what they said. What you have done is *hear*, not listen.

Listen for the speaker's intended meaning, not for what you are hoping to hear. You may fall into the pattern of expecting to hear particular things – whether it be particular client concerns or issues, topics of interest, points of view and so on. Once you hear what you're expecting to hear, you stop listening as your own beliefs have been confirmed. You attach your own meaning to what is being said, rather than taking in the speaker's meaning. Stephen R Covey, author of *The 7 Habits of Highly Effective People*, said, 'Most people do not listen with the intent to understand; they listen with the intent to reply.'[79] When you do listen, *listen to understand*.

To listen to understand you must listen to the meaning behind the words, as well as to what's *not* being said. Richness of meaning can come from listening to the unspoken. As Peter Drucker said, 'The most important thing in communication is hearing what isn't said.'[80]

You can increase your level of understanding by noticing the following when you speak with others:

- What agendas or concerns are not being expressed, yet are fundamental to what is being said?
- Do you understand the speaker's meaning-making – their values, beliefs, concerns and agendas?
- Are you paying attention to the speaker's nonverbal communication (facial expressions, gestures and tone of voice) to add meaning to the spoken words? Does the nonverbal

communication match the words they are saying, or is it telling you something else?

- Can you sense the emotions the other person is expressing through the passion they convey, the speed at which they talk or the style of language they are using? The same words can mean different things depending on context and expression.

When you really care about the other person and demonstrate empathy through careful listening, you can stand in their shoes and understand their point of view. This will only come through listening to them before you jump into solution mode. Empathising with another person deepens your relationship; you learn more from each other and see and hear the other person's perspective.

Self-coaching exercise

Following your next meeting, note down what you learnt from the conversation by completing the columns in Table 9.

Table 9: Conversation learnings

Meeting date	Attendees' names	What did I learn from what was said?	What was the meaning behind the words (what wasn't said)?

How to show you are listening

When you are really listening, you are making room for someone else to do the talking. The best leaders are those who demonstrate that they are present and engaged while the other person speaks. There are several techniques you can use to show you are actively listening.

Eye contact and body language

Eye contact is the easiest way to demonstrate your engagement and show that you are attentive and present. Don't have your eyes glued to the notes you are taking, and don't look away from or past the speaker. It's important not to overcompensate, though, by staring intently as you focus on each word the other person is saying. Maintain a culturally appropriate level of eye contact.

Be especially mindful of eye contact when you're using video technology. Line your computer camera up so that it sits at eye level, and speak and listen with the camera in mind. A computer stand or pile of books will do the trick to lift your computer to the appropriate height.

My coachee Ruchi always uses two computer screens. Ruchi had her camera on her laptop, yet spoke to me on her larger screen – meaning we couldn't maintain eye contact, which made it more challenging for me to read her facial expressions. I asked Ruchi if we could try an alternative set up where she spoke back to the screen with the camera. I shared with her that it made such a difference to how I listened. I was able to learn much more from her by seeing her facial expressions.

Video technology provides us with a direct view of our listeners. It's clear when they are multitasking by reading emails (their eye movements and the change of light reflecting on their face are giveaways), and when they are distracted by other things happening beyond the camera. Video technology doesn't provide us with the peripheral vision we would have if we were located in the same room as the person we're speaking with, so we can't determine whether they are listening while altering their gaze or whether they are distracted and not listening. In the absence of this wider vision, doubt about the person's level of attention can arise.

Facial expressions and other body language, such as gestures, can help to demonstrate your presence. A nod, smile, hand gesture or similar can show you are in sync with the other person. This too can be achieved using video technology. Most importantly, turn your video on! It's so much harder to listen well when you're talking to an avatar.

Vocal cues

Using vocal responses, such as 'mmhm' and 'uh-huh', communicates that you are listening to and hearing the other person. Be careful not to interrupt unnecessarily, though. Simple vocal cues can be supportive.

Reframing

Reframe or use reflection to let the person know you have heard them. You can paraphrase or restate what they've said in your own words. For instance, you might say something like, 'From what you've just shared I understand that X, Y and Z are critical concerns for your business right now. Have I understood you correctly?' Or you could be more direct and mirror what you've heard, saying, 'So, what I'm hearing you say is…'

Reframing ensures that you are on the same page as the speaker and have understood what they are saying and what is important to them. This gives you a chance to clarify what you have heard and demonstrates that you are moving towards a shared understanding.

Avoid distractions

Remain present with the speaker and try not to lose concentration. This can be best achieved by avoiding attending to your phone and email during the conversation. Avoiding multitasking is such an easy way to show that you are fully present and attentive. It's awful speaking to people who are playing with their phone as you speak. You find yourself speaking to the top of their head as their eyes are lowered to their glowing screen.

I often suggest to my coachees that it's better to let someone know that now is not a good time to talk than to drift in and out of the conversation. Explain that you are busy working on another priority, and you want to be present with them when you're talking to them, which will be a challenge at this time. Propose an alternative time to talk with the person when you can give them your full attention.

During a conversation you may become distracted by what is popping up in your head, or even by the way the person speaks. Their use of filler words such as 'um' and 'ah' or their repetition of particular words or catchphrases might distract you. My coachee Kai used to habitually say 'right' at the end of his sentences. For instance, he'd say 'This happened… right. Which means that I can't take that opportunity… right?' This became distracting for me, and I had to actively work to overlook it so I could focus on the substance of what was being said.

Taking notes can be a useful technique to capture what you are listening to while helping you maintain focus and avoid distractions. Asking someone if they mind if you take notes can help them understand why you are tapping away or looking down at your notebook.

Self-coaching exercise

Reflect on whether you used any of the following techniques in your last conversation:

- Eye contact
- Body language (nodding or shaking your head, smiling, frowning, hand gestures and so on)
- Vocal cues
- Reframing.

What distractions interfered with your ability to listen? Take a moment to note them down in Table 10 (overleaf) and include how you might mindfully counter these next time.

Table 10: Distractions and actions to counter them

	✓	✗	Action to counter distraction
Mobile phone alerts			e.g. Turn off your phone, put it on silent or put it away.
Email notifications			e.g. Turn off notifications or close your computer during the conversation.
Distracting thoughts			e.g. Focus on the speaker to learn from them. Jot some notes as they speak to hold your attention. If this is not possible, reschedule the conversation.
Fatigue			e.g. Suggest a break for coffee. Reschedule if you are unable to overcome your fatigue.
Challenges hearing the speaker			e.g. Adjust your position, or bring the issues to their attention so they can modulate their sound.
Getting lost in their reply			e.g. Ask for clarification and let them know it's not clear for you. Try to be specific about what has confused you.
Other people (such as other team members seeking your attention)			e.g. Remain present with the speaker and ask other team members to connect with you once the speaker has finished talking. Close chat functions on your computer and turn away from distractions.
Outside noise or distractions			e.g. Alter your location to better engage in the conversation.
Multitasking			e.g. Stop!
Something else (note what it was)			

Get comfortable with silence

Here's a fascinating fact: the word 'listen' contains the same letters as the word 'silent'. What a gift! Get comfortable with silence; it's such a powerful listening tool. It allows space for everyone to digest what has been shared and leaves room for additional thoughts to develop. As comedian Jerry Seinfeld said, 'When you interrupt, you've stopped listening. People need to be heard.'

If you are a person who regularly fills the silence, throw this strategy into your virtual backpack. Count to three in your head before you enter the conversation to see whether others want to offer their perspective first. My International Coaching Federation Coaching Supervisor shared with me the acronym WAIT (Why Am I Talking?) to help me assess my engagement in a conversation. You can ask yourself this question when you're tempted to jump in with your own opinion rather than pausing to consider what has been said, and perhaps gain a new perspective.

It's important to consider how appropriate the decision to be silent is for the situation and the people you are listening to. My coachee Dona always used to speak last; she used to WAIT. This was a very intentional strategy that she adopted, as she recognised the benefits of using silence as a conversation listening tool. She would sit in silence while her team contributed to the meeting, intending to empower them to share their points of view rather than being driven by her views. She wanted her team members to have space to contribute without being influenced by her more 'senior' views. She wanted them to feel heard and valued.

Dona and I had an interesting coaching conversation in which we questioned the unintended consequences of doing this with her group. Was it possible that some of her less-experienced teammates may have felt intimidated by her silence? Did her desire to speak last create a point of tension in meetings, potentially affecting others' ease of participating? Did her long-lasting silence curtail the conversation as team members closed down in the hope that she would *finally* contribute? Dona hadn't considered these questions previously so this presented a new lens to look through. By considering the impact of your silence, you can consciously weigh up the intended and unintended consequences and make an informed choice as to when to re-enter the conversation.

Assess your listening skills

An easy way to assess your listening skills is to ask your close friends and family members for their thoughts. They'll surely enlighten you if they haven't already. If they tell you you're not a good listener and that comes as a surprise to you, perhaps it's true. Perhaps you just haven't tuned in and noticed. It might be a blind spot.

There are a few signs to look out for to increase your self-awareness around your capacity to listen. Noticing these signs requires you to pay attention to yourself and be mindful as you engage in conversations with others.

Are you being curious and inquiring of the other person, or are you always telling them what you believe they need to hear? If you're always 'telling', this is not conversing; it may mean you miss listening and learning opportunities. You may be listening with the intent to reply rather than understand.[81]

Are you creating a dialogue rather than just informing people? The difference is critical. Dialogue is when numerous parties share insights and information with unlimited boundaries. Dialogue engages others in a broader conversation beyond simply informing people of what you know. Telling people what you know can be very one-sided and leave little room for you to demonstrate how you listen.

Creating dialogue requires you to be a good listener. It consists of more than the sum of the individual parts shared in a conversation. In other words, dialogue is more than just you telling me something (a part of the conversation) and me responding with independent thoughts (the other part of the conversation). Dialogue is what emerges from the sharing of perspectives. It's something that develops from your exploratory stance. When you're in that stance, you enter with curiosity and inquiry and an openness to learn and create.

Consider whether you are engaging in an exploratory conversation, inviting others to share their thoughts and together creating multiple perspectives that can be synthesised into a common understanding.

In all of this there's a simple message to remember: you have two ears and one mouth. Be sure to use them proportionately.

Self-coaching summary

♦ The best leaders listen and broaden their perspective, insight, understanding and connectivity with those around them.

♦ Build your self-awareness of how well you listen to improve your impact.

♦ Assess what you are listening for. Selective listening limits your ability to hear what the other person is truly communicating.

♦ What is the meaning of what you have heard? What is the meaning of what has *not* been said?

♦ Notice how you demonstrate your listening using questioning techniques, verbal cues, eye contact, body language, reframing and silence.

♦ Notice what distracts you when you are listening, and select actions to overcome these.

♦ Listen to learn.

Practice 11

Conscious communication

'Abrupt? I don't think that's fair,' Dom said. 'Why would they have said that?' Dom was a little angry and disappointed in this feedback he had received from his leader after a recent presentation to the board. 'He said I spoke over people and was dismissive towards the board members,' explained Dom. 'I don't agree! I was simply passionate and had a lot to say. I mean, they'd only allocated me ten minutes. What were they expecting? I had to give them all the detail or they simply weren't going to see what I could see!'

Dom wanted to be transparent when describing the performance of the business he managed. He felt it was important to be honest so board members could understand why the business was performing as it was and what support it needed.

Dom had arrived at the board meeting with a detailed PowerPoint deck, with each of the ten slides filled with data and insights. Much time had gone into preparing this deck, and it demonstrated many of the projects that were in play at the time. Dom knew the deck intimately, having mulled over the possible questions the board members might ask. It was fair to say that Dom had built up this moment in his mind and had some underlying anxiety about presenting to them. He was generally comfortable speaking to others but harboured worries about others' opinions.

Dom and I had a revealing conversation as we talked through the situation. Dom reflected on his underlying anxiety and desire to land the presentation and impress the board. He also knew that when he was nervous he tended to speak quickly and enthusiastically. 'It could perhaps be interpreted as a little abrupt', Dom reflected. His zest may have caused him to jump in and offer further insights and bring the board members' attention back to what *he* thought was important in the slide deck. Perhaps he had missed some of the nuances of their questions and overlooked some of their perspectives. 'I guess that could be interpreted as dismissive,' Dom said.

Dom deflated as we spoke. He realised his communication style may have gotten in his way. He uncomfortably disclosed that this was not the first time he had received this kind of feedback. Perhaps he needed to pay attention to how he communicated and his impact.

How you speak to others can significantly affect your relationships. Your choice of tone, language, volume, pace and pitch all influence the impression you make in the moment and the impression that endures in your absence.

Dom and I set to work on a coaching strategy to support his communication with others. I'll share it with you now to add to your backpack of self-coaching strategies.

How are you communicating?

Dom and I started with a self-reflection exercise focusing on drawing attention to how he was communicating.

As a leader you must engage with others through many forums and mediums. How you communicate through these forums is of great importance. Improving your impact may require you to finesse your communication style to increase engagement.

Face-to-face communication needs to be treated differently to digital communication, in which humour and tone is not as obviously transferred, which can cause misinterpretation. Take stock of your audience to fine-tune your communication style. Are you speaking to a room full of people, a smaller group or one-on-one? Are you communicating in person or over video? Are you communicating verbally or in writing? Each requires different approaches to meaningfully engage, inspire and motivate others.

How you are communicating is often shaped by the message you are hoping to deliver. This takes some planning. If you shoot from the hip, you may fumble your way through your messaging and perhaps miss the mark.

Self-coaching exercise

The next time you need to deliver an important message, find time to plan your delivery and work through the following questions:

- What do you want to share?
- Why is it important?
- How can you deliver your message succinctly and specifically?
- What outcome are you hoping for?

Language matters

As a leader your voice is amplified, so you must be conscious of the language you use. Choosing the right words will have a significant impact on the effectiveness of your message. Being flippant versus deliberate can have many unintended consequences. Intentional communication – where you match your language to your intention – is an easy way to avoid confusion and regret.

Keep it simple

Specific communications are easier to understand than those that are too complex. Don't lose your message in complex language, acronyms or 'business-speak'. Don't forget that your audience may be a mix of those in the know and those who wish to know. Using unfamiliar terminology or buzzwords can cause audience members to disengage, restricting inclusion to a select few.

A useful practice is to write down the three key points you hope to convey in your communication and consider how you can speak simply to those points. Thoughtful communication is more impactful. In addition to the three key points, provide context to the topic rather than assuming that your audience is already on the same page as you. Context can prevent misunderstanding, making your communication more efficient.

Notice nicknames

I've worked with leaders who use nicknames. I've often found it challenging to use these nicknames, particularly when I do not have a personal relationship with the leader. It can sound cliquey when leaders reference co-leaders and team members by nicknames, particularly if those people are not known by those names by everyone. It can feel exclusionary to some and appear to favour others.

My coachee Divesh was uncomfortable using his co-leaders' nicknames. He knew of JT and Tommo, as well as Smithy and Labs, but he was reluctant to refer to them with this level of familiarity. He wanted to build relationships with them, but felt on the outer because he used their formal names while everyone else used their nicknames.

Consider the perception the use of nicknames may create in your communications. Is it necessary to address people by their nicknames in broad settings, or would it be more appropriate to refer to them by their formal names to ensure everyone knows who you are referring to?

Keep in mind that a nickname may not be appreciated by the person receiving it. Nicknames can be foisted on people – sometimes to anglicise or avoid mispronouncing a name. The recipient may feel uncomfortable addressing this.

As an alternative, be vulnerable and share that you are unsure how to pronounce their name. Ask for help as you seek their direction.

Practise saying their name to become more at ease in correctly pronouncing it. Write down the name phonetically to help you recall the pronunciation until you build your habit of saying it correctly. You can also ask your team member to advise what their preferred name is rather than imposing a shortened version on them. Names talk to our identity. Correctly pronouncing people's names makes them feel like they matter and are of significance. Lead the way in stopping to inquire and demonstrate how to make team members feel important and included.

Use gender-inclusive language

Using language that is friendly to all genders is motivating to others and role models appropriate behaviour. Mindful attention to this can create an inclusive workplace where all team members feel that they can bring their authentic self to work and be recognised appropriately.

You are not royal

Some leaders speak with an inflated sense of self by speaking in the first-person plural (with apologies to the royals). Doing this communicates self-importance and that you perceive yourself to have an elevated status, which alienates you from your team members. Remember, as a leader you are a part of the team. Be mindful that your language does not separate you from others.

Delivery matters

In Practice 10 I shared a powerful quote from Maya Angelou: 'People will forget what you said, people will forget what you did, but people will never forget how you made them feel.' How you deliver your message impacts how people feel when they receive it.

Start with empathy

Stand in the shoes of those you are communicating with to assess how your message might be interpreted and experienced. How might it make them feel? This is so important to do; it is often not so much what you say or how you say it but how you have made people feel that is enduring. Have you made them feel fearful, embarrassed, humiliated or concerned? Or perhaps they feel motivated, hopeful, interested and curious? You have control of how you make people feel through your communication.

Notice your emotions

If you appear stressed or anxious, your audience will feel your nervous energy. If you are overjoyed and elated, this will likewise transfer to your audience. Emotions are contagious and spread very quickly when leaders communicate – whether to a large or small group. Your emotions will affect others in a one-on-one conversation just they will with a larger audience.

Intentional breathing can support and centre you. It can help you focus your attention and slow down your heart rate, stabilising you in those anxious or energetic moments. Take some deep breaths before you speak to gain control of your emotions and continue to remain conscious of your breathing as you continue. My coachee Dom employed this technique to slow down his delivery by stabilising his overzealous energy.

Self-coaching exercise

You too can build this skill by using the following box breathing technique:

- Take a deep inhale through your nose for four seconds.
- Hold your breath for four seconds.
- Exhale through your mouth for four seconds.
- Hold your breath for four seconds.
- Repeat three times to slow yourself down and increase your attentional focus.

Notice how you are speaking

What does the delivery of your communication say to others? Are you speaking too quickly and making others feel challenged to keep up with your thoughts? Is your tempo too slow, making people feel bored or fatigued? Pausing too often can draw out your communication and make it challenging for others to remain present with you. Is your messaging confusing and scattered, or too blunt? Does your use of humour engage and lift others, or does it suggest you lack understanding of the issue's importance?

Set yourself up for successful dialogue and think about what you are contributing. Are you pouring too much information into your audience member's cup? Are they watching it overflow, unable to absorb all of what you are sharing? Or are you topping them up and leaving them some room to balance what's within their cup, ensuring they are not overloaded? Are you emptying their cup by draining their ideas without replenishing them? Think of the impact you are having as you engage in your dialogue.

Reflect on your level of comfort in public speaking. For some it comes easily. For others it is gut-wrenching. If you experience social anxiety when speaking in public, invest in a coach who can help you develop some public-speaking skills. It can do wonders for your confidence. Don't be too proud to do this. I've seen some leaders develop from being nervous presenters to skilled and engaging presenters after working with coaches who specialise in this area.

Prepare, practise and position

To make yourself and others feel most comfortable, make sure you prepare, practise and position your communication.

First, diarise time to *prepare*. The best leaders prepare what they want to say very deliberately.

Preparation helps you speak with ease, simplicity and clarity. Think about the outcome you desire and consider what needs to be communicated to achieve this. Is it a motivational rallying of the team? Is it an informational, town-hall-style presentation? Is it a smaller meeting requiring focus and direction? Is it a persuasive presentation with strategic intent? In all cases consider how you want the recipients to feel and prepare your thoughts and language towards that goal.

Preparation also includes visualisation. Use your mind's eye to visualise who you will be speaking to, what the environment may look like, where you may be located within the room and so on. The more that you visualise, the greater your opportunity to consider what could arise that might derail you. This preparation supports you to continue with confidence if the worst does happen, as you'll have prepared for the possible occurrence.

My coachee Simone wanted to meet with her team to share the new strategy that was being adopted. As part of her preparation she visualised how different team members might respond to what she was saying. Most would be open to learning, but she identified two team members who may oppose her message. She was concerned that their commentary might negatively impact others in the room. By visualising this situation, Simone prepared herself for possible interjections and was better equipped to respond when they occurred.

Visualisation can help you prepare for all sorts of potentially derailing moments, even those that occur online – including internet failures, slides not synching, people unexpectantly coming off mute, comments in the chat and being spoken over. If you're speaking in person you might, like Simone, visualise how your audience could respond to you. You might visualise how you will hold their attention and how you will respond when they cut you off, interject with a question or tell you there is limited time left. How will you respond if someone tries to shut you down through counterargument, or if people appear not to be listening? Consider the many permutations that may destabilise you in the moment and imagine how you might respond. This preparation will increase your confidence and reduce your chances of being derailed in the moment.

Practising your delivery is another important task that should be diarised. We've all witnessed great leaders speaking with confidence and intent. Those leaders have likely invested in preparation and have practised their presentation.

You can be very effective as a communicator if you know what you want to say and have heard yourself say it aloud. Speech sounds very different in your head to the spoken word. Practise aloud so you can finesse your key points and feel comfortable that you have the right language in mind to successfully share your message. This will buoy your confidence.

Finally, find a *position* that allows you to ground yourself as you present. This of course depends on the size of the audience you are engaging with. Some find it useful to have a lectern to mount themselves behind. Others like to speak with cue cards in hand to reference the key points they wish to share. You can consider variations when meeting with smaller groups; for instance, are you most comfortable sitting down or standing up? Be sure to have practised what feels most comfortable, as this will steady you as you speak.

Communicating feedback

A transformational leader provides timely feedback to their team members to help them learn and grow. To lead your way and have a sustaining leadership impact, you need to take responsibility for what you are communicating in those moments. Overcommunication can be distracting and confusing, while a lack of transparency opens the possibility for conjecture. There's a fine line to adopt in getting this right; it's possible you may need some trial and error to find a balance.

Reflect on the communication styles outlined following to see if any resonate with you.

I'm with you all the way

This leader is constantly communicating and providing feedback. Each step their team advances inspires this leader's commentary: 'Yep, that's what I would have done. Well done. Keep going,' or, 'No, don't do it like that, do it like this...'

If this is your communication style, consider how you may be stifling your team. Having you lead by their side is less than empowering. It may feel more like micromanagement. It can also lead to a dependence on your approval at each step, slowing down the team's advancement towards your shared goals. It stifles original thought and diversity. Your team members may become stuck as they await your feedback and lose their independence and initiative to continue without your continued approval.

Step back and select timely moments or milestones to communicate feedback. If in doubt, agree to these points in time with your team members so they can expect independence in between.

Tough love

This leader gives feedback directly and bluntly. They may not perceive or be sensitive to their team members' needs; as a result, feedback can feel like it's being delivered like a blow to the chin. While the recipient manages the sting they are less likely to appreciate, or necessarily hear, all of what the leader hoped to share.

This leader is likely to suggest that it's in people's best interest to receive direct feedback. 'They need to know, so I'll tell them. They won't change unless they know'. The expression 'you've got to be cruel to be kind' speaks to acting in a way that may seem harsh yet will ultimately benefit the recipient.

While this leader may have good intentions, the brutal honesty of their communication may shock and upset the recipients, leaving them feeling less than inclined to positively work towards change.

If this is your preferred style, reflect on the consequences of this form of communication.

Sugar-coating

This leader knows they have to communicate feedback, but they don't want to upset or disappoint anyone. They want their team members to like them and be engaged and motivated, so they dance around the feedback, hoping their team members have understood what they have communicated. This leader may be indirect, sandwiching the negative feedback between positive statements. This mutes its effect. For instance, the leader may say, 'You're doing really well. If you didn't mumble we'd be able to better hear your contribution. But we're really pleased with how you are getting on.' They use language that reflects on sub-par performance more positively than it should, diluting the important message. Yet, in their mind, they have communicated the feedback. It's now on their people to improve!

If this is your style, you may be slow to communicate feedback because you're trying to avoid the challenge, which can frustrate those who are relying on your action. The time lag between the issue occurring and the feedback being delivered might make the feedback less relevant and impactful.

When you sugar-coat feedback you limit its effectiveness. Leading with kindness isn't only telling people what they want to hear. It's about skilfully sharing insights with people to draw attention to the behaviours, emotions and thoughts that are not setting them up for success. If you want to support and develop others, be fair to them by ensuring that your message is clear. Don't hope that they have picked it out of what you have said and amplified it to the right level of importance.

Sharing feedback in an honest yet compassionate manner ensures you're drawing people's attention to the impact you desire. Being kind means your intention matches the impact. If you want someone to learn from feedback, you must be kind in sharing areas for development in a manner that allows them to consider and process the feedback, rather than sugar-coating the message or shocking them with blunt, heartless feedback.

Self-coaching exercise

In your notebook, reflect on the feedback you have given your team members during the last month. Note the style you adopted. Were you with them all the way, giving tough love or sugar-coating the feedback?

Consider the consequences and effectiveness of the feedback you delivered and make a note to assess how the person has progressed in light of your feedback. You might need to adapt your feedback delivery; keep reading to find out how.

Adopting radical candour

Radical candour is a communication technique developed by Kim Scott that involves a combination of caring personally and challenging directly.[82] It encourages you to communicate with a focus on the positive without ignoring the negative by understanding how your communication is landing with the other person.

Radical candour requires you to clearly communicate what needs to be improved as well as outlining the support that might be available to assist the person. It requires you to contextualise the feedback so the impact on the recipient and others is clear. Radical candour will help you positively support your team members' growth and development while role modelling an effective communication style.

My coachee Adrianne shared how she used radical candour to communicate feedback to her team member Charles. She explained what was working well and what he needed to focus on to improve his performance. She clearly outlined the areas of his performance, focusing on the behaviours rather than his personality traits.

Specifically, she wanted Charles to take the lead in meetings and have a bigger leadership presence. Charles was always very vocal *outside* of their meetings, yet relied on Adrianne to take the lead and contribute *within* them. Even when Adrianne made space for him to participate, his tendency was to swiftly summarise what she had said, rather than demonstrate his expertise and leadership in shaping the conversation further. Instead of telling Charles that he was not adequately participating in meetings, Adrianne was specific in communicating how he could be more effective as a leader by speaking up in meetings and sharing his point of view.

She reminded him of his subject matter expertise and the value he could bring to others by contributing. She communicated that she cared personally about the realisation of his strengths, which she believed would build his confidence.

Adrianne also wanted to directly challenge Charles's behaviour. She shared the consequences of his performance, providing examples of when he missed opportunities to contribute and teach others. She explained the impact of his silence: it reduced others' perception of his expertise and, as a result, he was overlooked for development opportunities. His lesser contribution also reduced the diversity of thought and potential for collaboration within the team. It limited the learnings for him and the team, and reduced creative, exploratory thought.

Adrianne asked Charles how he felt about the lesser impact he was having. He responded that it was frustrating and disappointing. Through questioning, Adrianne helped Charles explore what this meant to him, how he felt and whether he understood the impact of his behaviours. In doing so, Adrianne was able to demonstrate care while also challenging him.

In seeking his agreement that he would interject more often with his thoughts and observations, Adrianne was also able to elicit what support Charles needed to more actively participate in future meetings. Together they created a plan to support his development, which further demonstrated that as a leader she cared personally about him.

Add the strategy of radical candour to your virtual backpack. Here's how you can draw upon radical candour when communicating feedback to your team members:

- Speak with kindness and challenge the recipient. Let them know that you care about them, using the feedback to communicate insights to challenge their performance. Your team will only improve if issues are brought to their attention in a productive manner.

- Provide context so they understand the impact of their behaviour, emotions or thoughts. Be factual rather than judgemental.

- Bring feedback to their attention in a timely manner.

- Be clear so there is limited risk of miscommunication.

- Use questions to involve them. Have them convey their understanding of what has been said and your expectations.

- Assist them in determining the support they require to advance.

Your role in facilitating quality communication

As a leader, the quality of your communication will be observed and emulated – more so the higher you progress in your organisation. If you model or tolerate poor communication you diminish the tone and tenor of the organisation. Your leadership impact may well be long lasting, but it will be far from positive. Command-and-control-style communication that demeans, diminishes or humiliates does not inspire or motivate. Your awareness of how you and others are communicating can improve the organisational climate and improve the collaboration, learning and innovation that results.

Quality communication is an essential factor in your team's ability to have a generative dialogue, where they collaborate and form new solutions as they learn from each other's contributions.[83] As a leader, you can help move your team from a conversation where they tell each other what they individually know to one that allows for respectful debate and where new perspectives are revealed (see Figure 11).

Figure 11: Facilitating quality communication

ADAPTED FROM C SCHARMER, 'FOUR FIELDS OF GENERATIVE DIALOGUE', *GENERATIVE DIALOGUE COURSE PACK*, 2003.

Allowing your team to stall in the 'tell' stage creates a highly prescriptive environment, with little room for others to contribute contrary thought. In this environment, people are speaking politely and are avoiding dissonance or disagreement. Conversations are filtered and people are careful not to offend. This form of communication is unlikely to lead to collaboration, as it diffuses others' opportunities to explore or refine what's been shared.

Moving to respectful debate requires you to create a culture of respect in which others' thoughts are shared, with the intention of assessing the quality of the contribution. As a leader, your role is to notice any judgements that become evident from your team during the debate and that hinder opportunities for collaboration. Bringing these to the attention of those in conversation can help to identify whether their judgements are curtailing their ability to listen and explore perspectives more widely. Team members' primary concern at this stage is convincing others of their point of view. It can be a combative space where team members are looking for contradictions and errors in others' ideas. As a leader, you have a role to play in moving the conversation beyond this stage to allow for greater collaboration.

Your leadership impact will grow when you nudge your team to reflective communication. In this stage the team will listen with empathy and inquiry to learn more from each other. They will use reflection and reframing to demonstrate a shared understanding, which builds trust between them. In this stage your team members can stand in others' shoes to understand why they might be holding a point of view. This enables broader insights to build across the team, which moves it towards collaboration.

The final step is to move your team to the 'explore' stage, where together they form a new understanding integrating their perspectives. This collaborative stance represents the group's collective, integrated thinking. It's now operating interdependently.[84]

How do you move your team from 'tell' to 'explore'? Your role as a leader is to notice, in a non-judgemental manner, the properties of the team as it functions, and to reflect this to the team so that the quality of conversation can be improved. You listen to your team members and reflect back to them what has been said, what has not been said and the rhetoric that might be blocking the conversation.[85] This might include noticing patterns of behaviour such as:

- poor listening skills
- people interrupting
- people dominating the conversation and precluding new thoughts and opinions
- power dynamics where 'groupthink' results and everyone leans into the group's dominant viewpoint
- inappropriate language or behaviour that inhibits inclusion
- poor use of time
- skewed agendas that limit new insights
- repetition of ideas
- reliance on a single person's contributions
- debate (dialogue is preferable)
- avoiding dissonance
- lack of empathy.

When you bring these patterns to your team members' attention, they become more insightful and better able to have open, exploratory conversations. You engender trust and collaboration. Understanding how these stages of communication work strengthens your influence and ability to shift team conversations towards collaborative, generative communications.

This is a big ask of you and takes much practice; but once you master your role in listening and shaping the quality of your team's communications, you will be impressed with how you enable collaboration.

Self-coaching exercise

In your next team meeting, observe the communication between your team members and reflect on the following questions in your notebook:

- *Listen* to the nature of the communication. Which stage does it sound like: tell, debate, reflect or explore?
- *Notice* the dynamics of the team. What patterns of communication are emerging? What can you bring to their attention to help them move towards exploration and generative dialogue?
- *Role model* reflective and exploratory communication to assist the team in learning from your leadership.

Self-coaching summary

- How you communicate as a leader has a significant impact on your leadership.
- Communicate consciously and with intent.
- Language and delivery both matter; keep it simple and inclusive, and prepare, practise and position.
- Communicating feedback using radical candour shows you care personally about others and will challenge them directly.
- Consider the quality of communication and support your team needs to move towards generative exploration to enhance collaboration.

Practice 12

Leading with kindness

I was heading home from work, driving my car over the Sydney Harbour Bridge with my usual radio show playing. I'm the kind of driver who enjoys sharing my journey with others – whether it be passengers whose company I can relish or people on the radio who entertain me. On this day I was in the car on my own when a conversation on the radio caught my attention.

The radio hosts, Will and Woody, were chatting with Hugh van Cuylenburg from The Resilience Project – an organisation delivering resilience programs to schools, sports clubs and businesses. Hugh was talking about kindness and its relationship with happiness. He spoke of research showing that when you do something nice for someone, your brain releases the hormone oxytocin, which makes you feels good. He spoke passionately about the power of this hormonal release and the benefits that come from the simplest of things. Even witnessing others do good deeds can stimulate the release of oxytocin.

Will caught on to the ripple effect of this – how it could spread from one person to another. Then Hugh challenged Will and Woody, along with their listeners, to generate 1000 good deeds. Every day for the following two weeks, listeners called in to share their acts of kindness. I looked forward to my daily drive home, keenly listening to the progress until it culminated at 1767 good deeds! The impact was so moving. I felt an emotional shift as I drove home each day and witnessed the joy of others' good deeds.

I was inspired to act. I considered phoning in to share examples of my good deeds, but I wanted to do more to perpetuate this approach – 1000 acts seemed out of reach for me on my own.

The Jewish New Year was the following week. I baked honey cakes to deliver to my closest girlfriends and their families to celebrate a sweet new year. Then it dawned on me. I decided to use the new year milestone to start my year of living and leading kindly, inspired by Will, Woody and Hugh.

Leading a life with kindness

The concept of acts of kindness that Hugh described resonated strongly with me, as an Executive Coach whose practice is grounded in positive psychology. I had studied and implemented positive psychology interventions during my career and recognised his suggestion around acts of kindness as one such intervention. I knew much research sat behind what he was suggesting. It occurred to me how simply I could make a choice to alter my life and the lives of those around me through a year of living and leading kindly. I set a goal to carry out an act of kindness daily for 365 days.

Leading a life with kindness brings joy along with so many other benefits. Your personal impact is likely to be more positive, which will benefit those around you. You'll draw out optimistic responses in others, lightening their mental load. You'll role model a belief system that supports others and focuses on the greater good, rather than a more insular self-focus.

By taking on an external view you will increase your awareness of others, deepen relationships, grow your curiosity and alter your perspective. You can shine the light on so much more when you lead with kindness.

Leading with kindness engages others at a more personal level. It is less about being transactional in your leadership and more about leading with authenticity. You build warmth, trust and followership more readily.

I love this advice from Nina Bhatia: 'Be tough on issues, but kind to people.'[86] Recognising how people treat others, particularly when no one else is watching, is a great litmus test to establish that person's true nature. Treating people with kindness, respect and tolerance is decent human behaviour. As leaders, it's even more important we treat others as we expect to be treated.

Encouraging your team members to bring their authentic selves into the workplace – and celebrating diversity of thought, abilities, race, culture, lifestyles, education and experience – promotes kindness. Leading teams in which everyone feels at ease in bringing their whole self to work, rather than having to conceal their true self for safety, creates a kinder working environment. It provides psychological safety and encourages people to be their best selves.

Kind leadership frame

Self-coaching strategies that turn your attention to leading with kindness will support your leadership impact, enabling a long-term positive effect on those around you.

With that in mind I created a frame for my year of living and leading kindly. It helped me to focus each day on enacting my year-long goal. You can utilise this frame as you lead your way. Let's take a look at each element of the frame.

Draw your attention to how you positively impact others

Purposefully increase your mindfulness in noticing the impact you have on others. Choose to savour the act of kindness so that you too benefit.

Remain externally focused

Ensure that your daily acts of kindness move beyond you. If you can make someone's day just that little bit better through an act of kindness, that would be a wonderful achievement and give you much pleasure. Take a broad view of those around you and notice how you could positively impact them. Notice how you feel about that person, and how the kind and perhaps unexpected gesture impacts you both. Do you feel more invested in them? Has your relationship deepened?

Move beyond business as usual

This initiative has to extend beyond business as usual (BAU). You must broaden your thinking and actions. Your challenge is to think beyond the BAU actions you would normally take – to widen your perspective around kindness and stretch yourself and your impact further.

You will learn how simple an act of kindness can be: giving an encouraging smile, stopping to chat to a new team member or writing a quick note of thanks. The smallest acts can have a significant positive impact.

Daily acts matter

A workplace study concluded that practising *everyday* prosociality (behaviours that are intended to benefit others) is both emotionally reinforcing and contagious – it inspires further kindness and generates feelings of pleasure in others.[87] Everyday prosociality is an unequivocally positive experience.

Like other habits, once in place, attention to daily acts of kindness benefits those performing and receiving them. As a leader, do not underestimate the impact of kind actions. The potential for contagion is exciting, and the ripple effect of prosocial acts of kindness should motivate you to do more to have a broader impact.

The personal benefits of acting kindly

The data is so rich it can't be ignored: acts of kindness increase life satisfaction.[88] Given we're only here once, who wouldn't want to be more satisfied with their life? Subjective happiness also increases when you count acts of kindness.[89] If you plan to lead with daily acts of kindness, you have every right to expect that your own happiness will be positively impacted.

My year of living and leading kindly ended with a final point of reflection. I had savoured the experiences I had and become more mindful of the acts I engaged in. I had extended myself and, at times, stretched my thinking in considering what I had done on a particular day that qualified as an act of kindness. I had experienced a range of emotions and states: wonderment in considering what might come my way during the day and what act of kindness might result; curiosity in contemplating the impact of the act of kindness; creativity in deciding what or how the act of kindness could be initiated and delivered. I grew as a result. This is an important realisation. As a leader, you want to continue to evolve, rather then feeling satisfied with your status quo. The need for personal growth is often understated.

My tolerance of uncertainty increased as I grew accustomed to starting most days not knowing what my act of kindness might be. I had to allow for opportunities to present themselves during the day. I became more aware and attuned to my behaviours, emotions and thoughts, and I became more present to what I was experiencing in the moment.

My listening skills developed as I focused on learning what mattered to others. This magnified my ability to respond with a meaningful and relevant act of kindness later, because I understood their needs and interests and could support them with kindness accordingly.

My acts of kindness supported me through the challenges of the pandemic, when anxiety and tensions increased. The positive emotional response I experienced from continuing with my acts of kindness supported my emotional state during this difficult time.

I feel that this way of being is now a part of me. I'm quick to identify and respond to opportunities to live and lead with kindness. My participation is far from monotonous, as every day brings something new and often unexpected, both to myself and the recipient of my kind act. It's a meaningful way of being.

Leading with kindness

Leading with kindness is not just about being nice; nor is it being 'soft'. It's leading with empathy and compassion, with awareness of your impact on others and the environment around you.

Leading with kindness involves tuning into your teammates' needs and capabilities, taking care and responsibility to support them in their success. Leading with kindness is a conscious engagement with other people to support them in being their best selves – whether that's in the manner you support people through challenging coaching conversations or how you develop your own skills for others' benefit.

The more you practise leading with kindness, the more you will become self-aware and conscious of your interactions with others, and the more you will shape the leadership shadow you cast. Your actions in leading with kindness and its contagious effect will contribute to a kinder world.

Building kindness through psychological safety

Once of the easiest ways for you to lead with kindness is to create psychological safety in your workplace. Psychological safety occurs when people feel accepted and respected. A psychologically safe space is one where you can show up as yourself – including your differences, your unique ideas and your voice – without being constrained by having to manage the impressions you make or risk humiliation or embarrassment.[90]

In his book *The 4 Stages of Psychological Safety*, Timothy R Clark defined psychological safety as:

> ... *a condition in which human beings feel (1) included, (2) safe to learn, (3) safe to contribute, and (4) safe to challenge the status quo – all without fear of being embarrassed, marginalized, or punished in some way.*[91]

Consider the impact of creating such a workplace. Your kindness in doing so will enable you and others to bring their best selves into the workplace, building self-determination and increasing impact. In Practice 3 we discussed that self-determination arises when you have a sense of belonging, can use and build your competencies and have autonomy. People who are high in self-determination have increased self-belief and self-confidence. This creates more positive emotions and feelings of hope and optimism, which contribute to their wellbeing. People are then better able to develop solutions to complex problems. They become more open-minded and broaden their pathway thinking, supporting goal attainment. All of this results from you leading with kindness.

You can deepen your understanding and application of Clark's four-stage model of psychological safety by considering its relationship with self-determination theory (see Table 11 overleaf). When someone feels included, they feel that they belong (relatedness). When someone feels safe to learn, they build their competencies. When someone feels safe to contribute and challenge the status quo, they build autonomy and their competencies.

Additionally, when someone feels psychologically safe, they will feel seen, heard and valued. They will feel like they add value and can contribute. They will feel like they matter and are of significance. When people feel that they matter, they feel happier, healthier and more interconnected with other people.[92] Making people feel like they matter is a powerful act of kindness.

Table 11: The correlation between psychological safety
and self-determination

Clark's model of psychological safety	Self-determination theory
Included	Relatedness
Safe to learn	Competencies
Safe to contribute	Competencies and autonomy
Safe to challenge the status quo	Competencies and autonomy

Let's look at some self-coaching strategies that will support you in building both psychological safety and self-determination in your team.

Included – build relatedness

When people feel included, they feel a sense of belonging or relatedness. This builds their interpersonal confidence, which in turn makes people feel at ease with others and more willing to relax, be themselves and contribute. The crux of inclusion is ensuring that you are being mindful of others. You can role model inclusion as you lead with kindness by adopting the self-coaching strategies we'll look at in this section.

First, it's important to *induct new team members into the team*. Include team members from day one; provide a road map showing the way forward and welcome them into your team. Joining a new team can be an anxiety-producing process even for the most confident of people. Helping people settle into your workplace is not only a kind gesture, but it will set them up for success. As their leader, ensure that you check in with them regularly and diarise time to meet with them in the days and weeks to follow. Be mindful of the honeymoon period coming to an end, and ensure they are well integrated into your team so their inclusion continues into the future.

Make sure you always *start with a hello*. How often do you walk past colleagues and fail to acknowledge them? Don't be too busy or important to engage. Start with a smile, a wave or a nod of the head to acknowledge their presence. The smallest of kind gestures can make team members feel included, yet the absence can be soul destroying.

As a leader it's especially important you *don't ignore the niceties*. Don't assume that everyone knows each other just because *you* know everyone in the room. In any situation in which team members, colleagues, customers or clients come together, actively introduce people. It's not enough to simply state someone's name – it doesn't explain why someone is there and why they matter. State their credentials and provide some background that draws out their purpose for participating. This can help people feel a sense of belonging, increasing their self-determination and confidence. It can also help them feel like they matter and are of significance. For example, you could say something like:

> *Talia is joining us today given her experience in marketing. She brings her creative thinking to our project and will help us examine and script the brief. Jared has experience in photography and has a keen eye for detail. I'm pleased to have him here to complement our team's crafting of the proposal with his photographic skills. Jessica is also joining us with her strengths in accounting. She will help us cost out the project.*

You should also *set expectations*. Let people know that you are hoping they will share their thinking during your meetings. By kindly inviting people to contribute, you can help them feel included.

During meetings, *make space* for everyone to contribute. Who are you hearing from and who hasn't yet contributed? I loved hearing of a CEO who used to attend meetings with pen and paper in hand. He'd list the attendees and, as they spoke, he'd put a small pen mark next to their name. This wasn't to try to intimidate but was a tool to help him notice who had a chance to share their point of view. It empowered him to invite those who hadn't yet spoken to do so. He would offer a simple invitation such as, 'Jane, you haven't yet had a chance to contribute. Is there anything you would like to add? I'm interested to hear your thoughts on this too.' This CEO effectively role modelled engaging and including others with kindness.

Be mindful of the challenges of participating in a meeting. If a team member is dominating the discussion, make some space for others to feel that they can contribute. This might mean you need to ask the eager contributor to pause for a moment while you hear from others. You could say something like, 'Thank you for your input, Jonathan, and for adding to our thinking. Could I ask you to pause while we hear from some of the team who are yet to share their thoughts? We'll return to you in a moment.'

Finally, it's important to *listen*. Use the techniques we learnt in Practice 10 to reframe, reflect and acknowledge contributions from others. It can be very uncomfortable when someone contributes to a discussion and no one acknowledges them. It's even worse if someone else suggests a similar idea soon after that *is* acknowledged! Be sure to make people feel valued, heard and included by being mentally present.

Listen to the language being used, and embrace gender-inclusive language so that everyone feels they can be present and part of the conversation.

Listen for what's important to your team members. Notice what they celebrate, honour and value and take an interest in them to better understand who they really are. Embrace diversity of thought, experience, culture and background to create a sense of belonging, inclusion and mattering.

Self-coaching exercise

Select three approaches from those outlined in this section to focus on inclusion during the next three months. Diarise weekly reflection sessions to assess what you have done differently and the impact of your actions. You are building new habits.

Discuss the exercise with a co-leader to share your insights and transfer your knowledge. Encourage your co-leader to replicate this inclusion exercise to ripple the impact of your focus on kindness and create greater psychological safety.

Safe to learn – build competencies

When you feel safe to learn you can build your competencies, which increases your knowledge and ability to add value through participation. As a leader, you can act with kindness in supporting your teammates with feeling safe to learn.

First, *adopt a growth mindset.* Create an environment where people focus on the process of learning rather than being fixated on the outcome. Quality communication is essential here; refer back to Practice 11 for further insights. You can role model exploring diverse perspectives and create a dialogue where team members collaborate in forming new ideas. Openly sharing information makes it safe to learn. Encourage team members to learn from each other and collaborate.

As a leader you must *support rather than rescue.* I use the phrase 'support, don't rescue' with my coachees who are high in empathy and tend to step in to assist their team members. As we learnt in Practice 9, while the urge to rescue may come from a place of kindness, it leaves less room for people's growth and development. Very little learning results from being rescued. Think about your actions. Refrain from simply telling your team member the answer when a challenge arises; help them to learn by coaching them through it. Kindness in leadership means supporting people to discover their options so they can support themselves in the future. Don't deny your people this learning experience.

It's also important to *create a learning culture* that fosters knowledge-sharing and professional development. Discuss the positive impact of personal growth and development and reinforce the opportunities it brings. Share your own learning, and support team members in plotting their growth journeys. Help them understand their strengths so they can draw on these as they learn. This can increase confidence, optimism, engagement and motivation.

Self-coaching exercise

Encourage everyone to maintain a learning mindset (where it is safe to learn and build their competencies) by asking the following questions at the end of each meeting:

- What have we learnt from our discussion today?
- What has been most meaningful to you?
- What else do we need to learn to take us forward?
- How will we discover more?

Safe to contribute – use autonomy and build competencies

When people feel safe to contribute, they can make a *choice* to participate and make a difference. They feel that their competencies will be recognised, and this builds their self-worth. They can feel that they add value through sharing their opinions, which makes them feel that they matter. They lean into bringing their best selves.

How can you kindly lead and make it safe to contribute? First, *allow for mistakes*. Make people feel that it is okay to make mistakes when they're sharing ideas. Talk about the fact that, even in your role, you don't have all the answers; you need their support. Share that you don't always get it right, yet you continue to contribute until you do. Tell stories about situations when you have failed, and how you responded. Outline the steps you took to build your resilience and mental toughness to bounce back and respond to such challenges.

Next, *encourage curiosity*. The simplest way to make it safe to contribute is to encourage the team to ask questions. Knowing it's okay to ask questions can bolster team members' self-confidence and autonomy as they know they have permission to play. It increases their ability to control how they contribute and learn.

What happens when no one asks a question? Ask one out loud for them. Show them how to inquire and discover more. For example, you could say:

- 'I'm wondering, what's the relevance of this concept?'
- 'I've been wondering about how to make sense of this.'
- 'The question that puzzles me is...'
- 'What's your point of view in relation to this?'
- 'How would you use your prior experience in this case to unpack this problem?'

Role modelling in this way demonstrates kindness in leadership as you show them the way. By seeking their opinions you are also showing them that they are relied upon and matter. It makes them feel relevant.

It's also important to model *gratitude*. Thanking people for their contribution can be a kind way to boost their positive emotional affect, which improves their wellbeing, motivation and engagement. This can make it feel safe to contribute and reinforce that their choice to contribute is positive. Practice 9 can support you with considering how you can effectively share gratitude with your team members.

As a leader, it is also your role to *create an even playing field*. Ensure that there is equity in the opportunities provided to contribute to. This might be as simple as running your eye over the names of presenters on a proposed panel or ensuring that there is diversity of representation in your leadership team. Perhaps it's assessing your team composition and noticing how similar or diverse the team is. If you identify that many people on your team have the same strengths, communication styles, backgrounds and interests, champion a program to hire for diversity.

Be mindful of how you create forums for contribution. Are you cognisant of the differing needs of your team – such as childcare, which prevents some from attending 8 am or 5 pm meetings, or accessibility, which challenges others from accessing particular meeting rooms? Are you aware of the differing communication styles within your team, including introverts and extroverts, and how this impacts participation?

If you strive to promote equity in your team you will make it safe for all to contribute. You will have recognised your team members' differing needs and created an environment that supports their ability to contribute and learn. This builds their autonomy and competency development. It also helps them to feel that they are of value and matter.

Self-coaching exercise

List your team members by name in your notebook. Note down their key strengths, communication styles and preferred work arrangements.

Assess the similarities and diversity of your team and consider how you are providing safety for them all to contribute. How are you ensuring that you are creating an even playing field? How are you being mindful of their capacity to contribute, and how can you provide opportunities for them to do so? How are you being attentive to their strengths and communication styles to enable them to safely contribute? How are you inquiring of their particular needs to support them in being their best selves?

Safe to challenge the status quo – use autonomy and build competencies

As you become more senior in your team your perceived status increases. Rightly or wrongly, team members may respect hierarchy and be deferential towards you. They may feel uncomfortable challenging you or other leaders and worry that doing so might be a career-limiting move. As a kind leader you can make it safe for your people to challenge the status quo.

As the leader, you can *go first*. Demonstrate your vulnerability, curiosity and openness to learning. Say, 'I don't have the answer. I'm keen to learn and find out.' As a leader, you may be a subject matter expert, but you can still adopt humility and display how keen you are to learn from others, as they should be to learn themselves.

Draw your team members in and ask for diversity of thought. You could say, 'Does anyone have a different view to the one I've presented? I'd like to learn from you,' or, 'Can you see another way to solve this problem that differs to my approach?' Once they start to engage, be encouraging and open to what has been shared.

You can also focus on *encouraging healthy and respectful debate*. I like the term 'respectful dissent'. Role model how this can be achieved so your team members can demonstrate divergent views. Invite team members to discuss alternative ways of solving problems. This can help your team move away from groupthink, which represents the status quo.

Re-read Practice 11 to learn how to help your team move the conversation from telling to debate to reflection and to exploration, where new perspectives are generated. Encourage collaboration, where multiple people join together to solve problems and create new outcomes. Focusing on innovation can help team members move away from the status quo and challenge its existence.

Self-coaching exercise

Consider how you can make it safe for others to challenge your views, and those of more senior leaders, by answering the following questions in your notebook:

- How can you use humour to diffuse any tension?
- How can you nudge others to recognise the faults in your logic?

- How can you encourage them to teach you and share more as an act of *their* kindness towards you and the other team members?
- How can you alter your team members' mindsets to remove any fear in challenging the status quo?

You have the ability to role model psychological safety as you lead. Each of the four stages elicits kindness in including others and allowing them to learn, contribute and challenge. Your leadership impact will be positive and sustaining when you ensure that your team is working in a safe and effective environment free from the risk of fear, embarrassment and humiliation.

Set kind business objectives

As a leader you may have the ability to influence the business objectives being set. Consider how you can do this with a kind mindset.

Ask yourself questions to test how you are influencing the work opportunities and environment for you and your team. Also consider whether the business objectives will benefit the wider community. Can you shape them so that your work contributes to a better world? You might develop policies encouraging engagement with certified sustainability suppliers, or policies that have a positive environmental impact in other ways, allowing for better governance and improved social responsibility.

Consider how you can demonstrate kindness through coaching and mentoring team members towards these business objectives. How are you supporting your people when they experience personal and professional challenges? Are you drawing on empathy and compassion to be a kind, human-centred leader? Are you sharing feedback to assist your colleagues with their professional development?

Consider what you are doing to create a kind work environment. Are you setting KPIs, metrics and goals for your team members that draw on their strengths and capabilities? Are you allocating reasonable time frames and resources to these goals to allow for their success? Are you role modelling what work–life integration looks like? Are you enabling flexible work practices to engage your team productively? Are you broadening your perspective to identify the changing system dynamics, noticing what is emerging in the systems around you? Are you being flexible and agile in your decision-making practices, supporting diversity of thought, experience, culture and background? Are you role modelling inclusivity and psychological safety? Are you using gratitude to demonstrate your appreciation of your team members?

Most importantly, are you leaving your organisation in a better state than when you first arrived?

All of this affects your ability to be a kind leader who leads with impact and has a positive, enduring legacy. What might you need to do more of to achieve this outcome?

Remember, 'No act of kindness, no matter how small, is ever wasted' (Aesop).

Self-coaching summary

♦ Leading with kindness creates a positive, enduring leadership impact.

♦ Kindness benefits you and others. It results when you:
  - draw your attention to how you positively impact others
  - remain externally focused
  - make it more than BAU
  - engage in daily acts of kindness.

♦ You can lead kindly and create psychological safety where everyone brings their whole self to work and feels included and safe to learn, contribute and challenge the status quo.

♦ You can lead kindly to make people feel that they matter and are of significance.

- Consider setting business objectives with a kind mindset. Reflect on what you're doing to leave your team and organisation in a better state than when you first arrived.
- No act of kindness, no matter how small, is ever wasted.

Conclusion

Look at the leadership muscles you've grown! Yes, you! Take note of how much you have learnt about yourself and others by reading this book. Your virtual backpack is full of self-coaching strategies to accompany you each day. Your mental capacity has grown with new insights, thoughts, practices and habits. You're sure to see the difference in your leadership stride.

Every new practice takes continued effort to become a habit. As you continue to lead yourself, consciously make use of the self-coaching strategies in your backpack. Regularly review your behaviours, emotions and thoughts to establish whether you are continuing to have the leadership impact you have been working so hard to have. It takes sustained effort, yet the benefits make it worth every moment.

I'm excited for what's ahead for you and your teams. Leadership is a journey. As you arrive at new leadership challenges, pause and search through your backpack to find the self-coaching strategy that aids you. You might need to reshuffle the backpack from time to time to bring alternative strategies to the top. At times you might be slower to grab a strategy and put it into action. When this happens, be kind to yourself and forgiving of any leadership hiccups that result. Learn from your mistakes and recognise the lifelong learning that is in place. Re-read the related chapter in this book and reflect on what it brings up for you. Notice your sense of wellbeing and the wellbeing of those you lead. How are you creating a positive experience as a connected, observant and authentic leader?

Here's the magical thing about your self-coaching backpack being virtual: you will always be able to make more space to add further helpful strategies to support you. What I have brought to your attention is not finite. There are plenty more worthwhile self-coaching strategies to adopt. Keep your mind open to learning more so you can continue your journey of self-awareness and self-improvement. When leaders make themselves available for learning and widen their perception, their understanding of themselves and those around them will grow. The ability to engage with diversity of thought, beliefs, experience and backgrounds will be more accessible. The world will become a better place as you lead in this way.

At the beginning of this book I expressed my hope that its contents would enable you to lead yourself and then lead others, creating a positive, enduring leadership impact. Your ability to achieve this has been heightened, and I am thrilled to think of the potential change you will bring. To increase the ripple even further, I'd be delighted if you shared my book with other similarly minded leaders. Help them understand how they can self-coach their way and have a positive leadership impact. If you have underlined, dog-eared and well-thumbed your way through your copy of this book, keep it on hand for ongoing reference and buy a copy or two for your fellow leaders so they can do the same.

Do keep in touch and let me know how you get on. Our journey is not complete – there are many more strategies to be shared. I would love to hear your feedback on my book and learn of other self-coaching strategies you might find supportive. Feel free to connect with me on LinkedIn and via my website:

linkedin.com/in/karen-stein-coaching
karensteincoaching.com

Blessings and love x

About Karen

Karen Stein is an Executive Coach with a passion for supporting leaders to be their best selves. After studying Economics and Law at university she continues to enjoy a 30-plus-year career in professional services, including 23 years as a Partner of Deloitte. The first chapter of her career was spent supporting organisations accessing funding solutions for furthering research and development within Australia.

As Karen moved towards her halfway point in life, she reflected on how she could live out her chapter two in an impactful way. At around the same time she was fortunate to be provided with a coach while on an executive leadership program and fell head over heels in love with the process of coaching. She knew coaching would allow her to support others to be their best selves, and her to do the same.

To step into this new world, she completed a Certificate of Coaching Practice, which was a lovely entree to completing a Master of Science in Coaching Psychology at the University of Sydney. In 2016, Karen pivoted into her second career within Deloitte as a Talent Partner and Executive Coach. She designed and implemented the Executive Coaching Program for Women Partners in Deloitte, which she has led since that time. It's her dream come true!

With over 2000 one-on-one coaching hours, and as an International Coaching Federation Professional Certified Coach, Karen provides executive leadership coaching to evolving senior leaders, supporting them to achieve their professional goals. She also co-facilitates leadership programs as a Partner faculty member of Deloitte University Asia Pacific, and as a part of the Partner Learning and Development team at Deloitte Australia.

Karen's experience as a senior leader within a professional services environment means she was for a long time on her coachees' side: a leader hoping to bring her best self to her team, her clients, her community and of course herself. She also wants to be a role model for her two amazing sons, Adam and Nathan, and her fabulous nieces and nephews: Jess, Lily, Rose, Avinoam, Daniel, Ma'ayan and Yarden. She hopes they will view leadership in a positive light and learn how to lead themselves as the young leaders and wonderful humans they are.

Karen is passionate about making a difference, empowering leaders to support themselves through their careers. She feels fortunate to work with inspiring leaders each day with varied backgrounds, goals, dreams and challenges. She also provides voluntary coaching to clients of Dress for Success and the social enterprise Bambuddha Group. She has supported the global coaching community as a Steering Committee Member of the Institute of Coaching APAC Round Tables. As a skilled listener, she is a true cheerleader of those she coaches and keenly works to make access to coaching more equitable for all.

Based in Sydney, Australia, Karen is known for baking delicious honey cakes. Her love of sweet treats is equal to her love of sharing interesting thought leadership.

Karen recently authored a chapter on mental toughness in the book *Coaching for Self Awareness About Attitude and Mindset*, published in the UK. You'll hear her as a guest speaker on podcasts, and see her presenting keynotes and writing and sharing articles with her network to enable those around her to live their best lives, be great leaders and ripple their impact to make this world a better place.

Karen hopes that this book will enable you as a leader to pause and reflect, and consider what your leadership impact is and can be. You too can positively impact our world.

Note of thanks

I've been fortunate to be surrounded by a most loving and caring family: my parents, Leslie and Clara; my brother Mark; my in-laws, Michael and Susan, David and Hedya; and, most special to me, my gorgeous and talented husband Andy and wonderful sons Adam, Nathan and Charlie the cavoodle. Thank you for your love and care, your interest and encouragement, and your humour and good counsel along the way.

My wonderful parents, being exceptional role models, teachers, thought leaders and published authors, have always supported me with a love of learning and a freedom to explore my interests and passions. They have instilled in me a quest for intellectual growth and development and, importantly, a deep care for family, friends, colleagues and the community.

My husband and sons have been my much-appreciated cheer-leaders, always encouraging me to get some more words on the page. They have engaged me in vibrant conversations, laughter, music and experiences that have broadened my understanding and perspective of the world we are in. They inspire me to be my best, and I hope this is reflected in this book. I am their biggest fan and love them to the moon and beyond!

I also benefited from teaming with my writing coach, Kelly Irving of the Expert Author Academy. Kelly provided a safe space to learn the art of writing and publishing. She took my understanding to a new level and introduced me to a wonderful community of like-minded authors, where we could all share our imposter thoughts as well as our excitement and joy. Writing your first book is scary and creates lots of space for self-reflection. I've loved the learning process I have been involved in with Kelly and the discovery of myself as an author. A big thanks to you, Kelly, for your support and guidance.

My thanks too to Lesley Williams, Brooke Lyons, Eleanor Reader, Will Allen and the rest of the team at Major Street Publishing, who have enabled this dream to become a reality! Your belief in my work is truly appreciated.

References

1. International Coaching Federation, *2020 ICF Global Coaching Study*, 2020, <coachingfederation.org/research/global-coaching-study>.

2. 'Chief', *Macquarie Dictionary*, <macquariedictionary.com.au>, accessed 2 March 2023.

3. S Sandberg, 'Sheryl Sandberg to Grads: Fortune Favors the Bold', *TIME*, 29 June 2015, <time.com/3939800/sheryl-sandberg-graduation-speech-tsinghua>.

4. Z Mercurio, *The Invisible Leader: Transform Your Life, Work, and Organization with the Power of Authentic Purpose*, Advantage Media Group, 2017.

5. Ibid.

6. Ibid.

7. Ibid.

8. AM Grant, 'An Integrative Goal-Focused Approach to Executive Coaching', in DR Stober and AM Grant (eds), *Evidence Based Coaching Handbook: Putting Best Practices to Work For Your Clients*, John Wiley & Sons Inc, 2006; A Duckworth and J Gross, 'Self-Control and Grit: Related but Separable Determinants of Success', *Current Directions in Psychological Science*, 2014, 23(5):319–325; B Höchli, A Brügger and C Messner, 'How Focusing on Superordinate Goals Motivates Broad, Long-Term Goal Pursuit: A Theoretical Perspective', *Frontiers in Psychology*, 2018, 9:1879.

9. AM Grant, op. cit.

10. Ibid.

11. NW Van Yperen, M Blaga and T Postmes, 'A meta-analysis of self-reported achievement goals and nonself-report performance across three achievement domains (work, sports, and education)', *PLoS ONE*, 2014, 9(4).

12. SK Johnson et al., 'Mastery Goal Orientation and Performance Affect the Development of Leader Efficacy During Leader Development', *Journal of Leadership & Organizational Studies*, 2018, 25(1):30-46.

13. RM Ryan and EL Deci, 'Self-determination theory and the facilitation of intrinsic motivation, social development, and well-being', *American Psychologist*, 2000, 55(1):68–78.

14. KM Sheldon, 'The self-concordance model of healthy goal striving: When personal goals correctly represent the person', in EL Deci and RM Ryan (eds), *Handbook of Self-Determination Research*, University of Rochester Press, 2002.

15. Ibid.

16. KM Sheldon et al., 'Self-concordance and subjective well-being in four cultures', *Journal of Cross-Cultural Psychology*, 2004, 35:209–223.

17. EL Deci and RM Ryan, *Intrinsic Motivation and Self-Determination in Human Behavior*, Springer Science & Business Media, 1985.

18. BL Fredrickson, 'The broaden-and-build theory of positive emotions', in FA Huppert, N Baylis and B Keverne (eds), *The Science of Well-Being*, Oxford University Press, 2005.

19. RM Ryan and EL Deci 2000, op. cit.

20. M Milyavskaya, D Nadolny and R Koestner, 'Where do self-concordant goals come from? The role of domain-specific psychological need satisfaction', *Personality and Social Psychology Bulletin*, 2014, 40(6):700–711.

21. L Legault, 'The Need for Competence,' in V Zeigler-Hill and TK Shackelford (eds), *Encyclopedia of Personality and Individual Differences*, Springer International Publishing AG, 2017.

22. A Behera and P Pani, 'Career and emotional self-awareness: Micro initiatives for macro impact', *Indian Journal of Positive Psychology*, 2014, 5(2):213–215.

23. T Eurich, *Insight: Why We're Not as Self-Aware as We Think, And How Seeing Ourselves Clearly Helps Us Succeed at Work and in Life*, Crown Business, 2017.

24. M Cavanagh, 'Coaching from a systemic perspective: a complex adaptive conversation', in DR Stober and AM Grant (eds), *Evidence Based Coaching Handbook: Putting Best Practices to Work For Your Clients*, John Wiley & Sons, 2006.

25. A Grant and J Greene, *Coach Yourself: Make Real Changes in Your Life*, Pearson Education, 2004.

26. A Behera and P Pani, op. cit.

27. M Dahl, 'Do You Have Any Idea What Other People Think of You?', *Science of Us*, 8 May 2017, <thecut.com/2017/05/do-you-have-any-idea-what-other-people-think-of-you.html>.

28. S Cox, 'Give the gift of feedback', *Nursing Management* (USA), 2016, 47(5):44–48.

29. T Eurich, 'The Specific Advice You Should Seek (and Ignore) to Become More Self-Aware', Quartz, 31 May 2017, <qz.com/993367/the-specific-advice-you-should-seek-and-ignore-to-become-more-self-aware>.

30. S Bellezza, N Paharia and A Keinan, 'Conspicuous consumption of time: When busyness and lack of leisure time become a status symbol', *Journal of Consumer Research*, 2016, 44(1):118–138.

31. CE Connelly et al., '"I'm busy (and competitive)!" Antecedents of knowledge sharing under pressure', *Knowledge Management Research & Practice*, 2014, 12(1):74–85.

32. T Buser and N Peter, 'Multitasking', *Experimental Economics*, 2012, 15(4):641–655.

33. RF Adler and R Benbunan-Fich, 'Juggling on a high wire: Multitasking effects on performance', *International Journal of Human-Computer Studies*, 2012, 70(2), 156-168.

34. JM Lahnakoski et al., 'Neural mechanisms for integrating consecutive and interleaved natural events', *Human Brain Mapping*, 2017, 38:3360–3376.

35. DP Ford, 'Disengagement from knowledge sharing: the alternative explanation for why people are not sharing', *ASAC*, 2008, 29(5).

36. JH Huh et al., 'I'm too Busy to Reset my LinkedIn Password: On the Effectiveness of Password Reset Emails' [conference presentation], *2017 CHI Conference on Human Factors in Computing Systems*, May 2017.

37. B Shuck and K Rose, 'Reframing employee engagement within the context of meaning and purpose: Implications for HRD', *Advances in Developing Human Resources*, 2013, 15(4):341–355.

38. S Sinek, *Start with Why: How Great Leaders Inspire Everyone to Take Action*, Portfolio/Penguin, 2013.

39. M Power (host), 'The Power of Purpose in Education, Work and Leadership, with Zach Mercurio', *Classroom 5.0*, Posify, 16 September 2021.

40. J Loehr and T Schwartz, 'The making of a corporate athlete', *Harvard Business Review*, 2001, 79(1):120–129, <hbr.org/2001/01/ the-making-of-a-corporate-athlete>.

41. Ibid.

42. K Richmond, '10 quick and healthy snacks to beat the 3pm energy slump', Cancer Council NSW, 7 April 2022, < cancercouncil.com.au/ news/10-quick-and-healthy-snacks-to-beat-the-3pm-energy-slump>.

43. E Svetlana, C Clerkin and MN Ruderman, 'Can't sleep, won't sleep: Exploring leaders' sleep patterns, problems, and attitudes', *Consulting Psychology Journal: Practice and Research*, 2017, 69(2):80–97.

44. CM Barnes, 'Sleep Well, Lead Better', *Harvard Business Review*, September–October 2008, 140–143, <hbr.org/2018/09/sleep-well-lead-better>.

45. J Orzel-Gryglewska, 'Consequences of Sleep Deprivation', *International Journal of Occupational Medicine and Environmental Health*, 2010, 23(1):95–114.

46. Centers for Disease Control and Prevention, 'How much physical activity do adults need?', 2 June 2022, <cdc.gov/physicalactivity/basics/ adults/index.htm>.

47. S David, *Emotional Agility: Get Unstuck, Embrace Change, and Thrive in Work and Life*, Avery/Penguin Random House, 2016.

48. Dalai Lama, *Beyond Religion: Ethics for a Whole World*, Houghton Mifflin Harcourt.

49. Based on an old parable; author unknown.

50. KJ Bao and G Schreer, 'Pets and Happiness: Examining the Association between Pet Ownership and Wellbeing', *Anthrozoös*, 2016, 29(2):283–296.

51. CN Armenta, MM Fritz and S Lyubomirsky, 'Functions of Positive Emotions: Gratitude as a Motivator of Self-Improvement and Positive Change', *Emotion Review*, 2017, 9(3):183–190.

52. K Neff, 'Self-Compassion: An Alternative Conceptualization of a Healthy Attitude Toward Oneself', *Self and Identity*, 2003, 2(2):85–101.

53. G Bernatzky et al., 'Emotional foundations of music as a non-pharmacological pain management tool in modern medicine', *Neuroscience & Biobehavioral Reviews*, 2011, 35:1989–1999; ML Chanda and DJ Levitin, 'The neurochemistry of music', *Trends in Cognitive Sciences*, 2013, 17:179–193.

54. M de Witte et al., 'Effects of music interventions on stress-related outcomes: a systematic review and two meta-analyses', *Health Psychology Review*, 2020, 14(2):294–324.

55. J Tseng and J Poppenk, 'Brain meta-state transitions demarcate thoughts across task contexts exposing the mental noise of trait neuroticism', *Nature Communications*, 2020, 11.

56 GL Flett, 'An Introduction, Review, and Conceptual Analysis of Mattering as an Essential Construct and an Essential Way of Life', *Journal of Psychoeducational Assessment*, 2022, 40(1):3–36.

57 Roy Morgan, 'It's official: Australians have more annual leave due than ever before', 17 December 2021, <roymorgan.com/findings/its-official-australians-have-more-annual-leave-due-than-ever-before>.

58 TD Allen et al., 'Career benefits associated with mentoring for protegee: a meta-analysis', *Journal of Applied Psychology*, 2004, 2(89):127–136.

59 Ibid.

60 TD Allen, E Lentz and R Day, 'Career success outcomes associated with mentoring others: A comparison of mentors and nonmentors', *Journal of Career Development*, 2006, 32(3):272–285.

61 C Hieker and M Rushby, 'Key Success Factors in Implementing Sustainable Mentor Programmes in Large Organisations', *International Journal of Evidence Based Coaching and Mentoring*, 2020, 18(2):197–208.

62 TD Allen, E Lentz and R Day, op. cit.

63 SG Baugh and TA Scandura, 'The effect of multiple mentors on protégé attitudes toward the work setting', Journal of Social Behavior and Personality, 1999, 14(4):503–522.

64 J Whitmore, Coaching for Performance: The Principles and Practices of Coaching and Leadership, John Murry Press, 2017.

65 SA Hewlett, Forget a Mentor, Find a Sponsor: The New Way to Fast-Track Your Career, Harvard Business Review Press, 2013.

66 J Taylor Kennedy and P Jain-Link, 'Sponsors Need to Stop Acting Like Mentors', *Harvard Business Review*, February 2019, <hbr.org/2019/02/sponsors-need-to-stop-acting-like-mentors>.

67 Deloitte Australia, *Sponsors* [internal document), 2020.

68 Deloitte, 'What projects will you—or should you—sponsor?', 2017, <https://www2.deloitte.com/us/en/pages/finance/articles/cfo-insights-four-sponsorships.html>.

69 J Taylor Kennedy and P Jain-Link, op. cit.

70 SA Hewlett, *The Sponsor Effect: How to Be a Better Leader by Investing in Others*, Harvard Business Review Press, 2019.

71 Ibid.

72 Ibid.

73 R Holmes, 'Reverse mentoring is the technique that helps managers as much as their employees', Quartz at Work, 16 February 2018, <work.qz.com/1206074/reverse-mentoring-is-the-technique-that-helps-managers-as-much-as-their-employees>.

74 D Morrison, 'Chief of Army message regarding unacceptable behaviour' [video], 12 June 2013, < youtube.com/watch?v=LhK7YxpdeNg>.

75 M Akinola, A Martin and K Phillips, 'To Delegate or Not to Delegate: Gender Differences in Affective Associations and Behavioral Responses to Delegation', *Academy of Management Journal*, 2018, 61(4):1467–1491.

76 L Waters, 'Predicting job satisfaction: Contributions of individual gratitude and institutionalized gratitude', Psychology, 2012, 3(12):1174.

77 RG Nichols and LA Stevens, 'Listening to People', *Harvard Business Review*, September 1957, < hbr.org/1957/09/listening-to-people>.

78 J Garvey Berger, 'Listening to Learn' [video], Cultivating Leadership, 25 July 2017, <youtube.com/watch?v=Zrg_3KlAE6o>.

79 SR Covey, The 7 Habits of Highly Effective People, Simon and Schuster, 1989.

80 S Ratcliffe (ed), *Oxford Essential Quotations*, 4th edn, Oxford University Press, 2016.

81 SR Covey, op. cit.

82 K Scott, *Radical Candor: Be a Kick-Ass Boss Without Losing Your Humanity*, St Martin's Press, 2017.

83 C Scharmer, 'Four Fields of Generative Dialogue', *Generative Dialogue Course Pack, 2003*.

84 MJ Cavanagh, 'The coaching engagement in the twenty-first century: New paradigms for complex times', in S David, D Clutterbuck and D Megginson, Beyond Goals: Effective Strategies for Coaching and Mentoring, Routledge, 2016.

85 Ibid.

86 J Reed, 'Be tough on issues, but kind to people – the leadership lessons of Nina Bhatia', REED, 28 January 2019, <reed.co.uk/james-reed/be-tough-on-issues-but-kind-to-people-the-leadership-lessons-of-nina-bhatia>.

87 J Chancellor et al., 'Everyday prosociality in the workplace: The reinforcing benefits of giving, getting, and glimpsing', *Emotion*, 2018, 18(4):507–517.

88 KE Buchanan and A Bardi, 'Acts of Kindness and Acts of Novelty Affect Life Satisfaction', *The Journal of Social Psychology*, 2010, 150(3):235–237.

89 K Otake et al., 'Happy People Become Happier through Kindness: A Counting Kindnesses Intervention', Journal of Happiness Studies, 2006, 7(3):361–375.

90 AC Edmondson, 'Psychological Safety and Learning Behavior in Work Teams', Administrative Science Quarterly, 1999, 44(2):350–383.

91 TR Clark, *The 4 Stages of Psychological Safety*, Berret-Koehler Publishers, 2020.

92 GL Flett 2022, op. cit.

Be better with business books

MAJOR STREET

We hope you enjoy reading this book. We'd love you to post a review on social media or your favourite bookseller site. Please include the hashtag #majorstreetpublishing.

Major Street Publishing specialises in business, leadership, personal finance and motivational non-fiction books. If you'd like to receive regular updates about new Major Street books, email info@majorstreet.com.au and ask to be added to our mailing list.

Visit majorstreet.com.au to find out more about our books (print, audio and ebooks) and authors, read reviews and find links to our Your Next Read podcast.

We'd love you to follow us on social media.

in linkedin.com/company/major-street-publishing

f facebook.com/MajorStreetPublishing

○ instagram.com/majorstreetpublishing

🐦 @MajorStreetPub